LURED
TO THEIR
DEATHS

LURED
TO THEIR
DEATHS

Trinity Mirror Media

Trinity Mirror Media

LURED TO THEIR DEATHS

By John Scheerhout

Published by Trinity Mirror Media in
association with The Manchester Evening News

First Edition
Published in Great Britain in 2013.
Published and produced by: Trinity Mirror Media,
PO Box 48, Old Hall Street, Liverpool L69 3EB.

ISBN: 9781908695185

Photography: Manchester Evening News, Mirrorpix, Christopher Foster,
Ian Caveney, Andy Stenning and GMP

Printed and bound by CPI Group (UK) Ltd, Croydon, CR0 4YY

Contents

Care of Police Survivors,
the North West Police Benevolent
Fund, and Victim Support have
been chosen to receive an equal share
of the proceeds from this book

Author's Thanks

Thanks are due to a great many people who helped me research and write this book, among them several police officers who felt able to contribute when their instincts were probably urging them to keep their counsel.

Without that help, it would have been a much more difficult and less credible exercise to undertake.

Fellow journalists at the Manchester Evening News and elsewhere, as well as members of the communities of Clayton and Droylsden, also provided invaluable support.

So, in no particular order, thanks to: Nick Adderley, Joanne Rawlinson, Dominic Scally, Simon Barraclough, Ian Hanson, Shelley Brierley, Michael DelRosso, Pete Bainbridge, Richard Wheatstone, Paul Britton, Dean Kirby, Pat Hurst, Kim Pilling, Emma Odell, Chris Brereton, Nicholas Clarke and Louise Brandon. There are others who I hope will forgive me if they have been missed off my list.

I am delighted that the proceeds from this book will support the charities named opposite, as chosen by the families of PCs Fiona Bone and Nicola Hughes. I cannot even begin to understand how they are trying to recover from their loss.

As an experienced journalist, all I can hope is that I have stayed faithful to the facts and provided an accurate account of the events which shocked and appalled every decent human being during the summer of 2012.

John Scheerhout

1.

A KNOCK AT THE DOOR

Dale Cregan's stubby, murderous fingers tapped away slowly on the keypad in front of him.

They were more used to pulling the trigger on his favourite Glock semi-automatic pistol or the firing pin on a hand grenade than typing on a laptop.

Eventually, his untrained digits spelled out the first word – 'life' – into Google, followed by the second – 'sentence'.

He sat back on the sofa and, through the cigar smoke, he considered the results on the screen in front of him. He knew his fate.

He had been on the run from the law for what felt like forever.

Watching, waiting, preparing.

LIFE

His startling police mugshot had stared out from wanted posters and the front pages of the newspapers for weeks.

With one eyeball missing, he had become a murderous, demonic Cyclops for a tremulous and frightened public.

However, instead of Cyclops' mythological thunderbolt, Cregan had used handguns and military grenades to strike fear into his many enemies.

The truth was, his grenades – or 'pineapples' as he affectionately called them – never actually killed anyone who wasn't already dead or dying.

Rather, they were gratuitous detonations, 'calling cards' designed to enhance his already fearsome reputation.

Just a few hours after his Google enquiry, Cregan would end one of the nation's biggest manhunts by simply walking into a police station.

But he would do so on his own terms, with the terrible sense of drama that became his trademark.

Yes, he would give himself up to the law. But he would go out in a blaze of heroic glory. Or at least that's the way he saw it.

Cregan had wearied of constantly looking over his shoulder, for the grass who might tip off the police for the £50,000 reward, for the enemies who wanted him dead, or for the hundreds of bobbies out looking for him.

The daily police visits to his mother had taken their toll on her, and now on him, and it was time to end it.

Not for him, though, a meek surrender. The killing was not yet complete. His black Glock, with its extended magazine loaded with 32 bullets, was beside him on the sofa.

A KNOCK AT THE DOOR

A hand grenade was also perched on the mantlepiece on the other side of the living room.

He was ready and waiting at the scene of his final and most outrageous act, a quiet, residential cul-de-sac in Mottram, a suburb just a few miles from the Peak District.

The residents of the village of Mottram in Longdendale – to give it its full title – had been completely unaware of the mysterious figure wearing a grey hooded top stalking their streets that night, searching for the perfect spot for his ambush. Underneath the hoodie and lurking in the shadows was Britain's most wanted man.

Cregan had grown a bushy full-face beard and he had become accustomed to moving around only at night to avoid capture.

Despite their widespread efforts, the police had not come close to finding him.

Unconfirmed reports suggested he had been brazen and confident enough to go drinking in local pubs.

If that was true, those who saw him had been too scared to dial 999.

He had been hiding all across the UK, and may even have spent some time sunning himself on Spain's Costa del Sol, protected by Russian gangsters, until he ran out of money and finally decided it was time to come home.

The hooded figure was thinking hard about how he would carry out his most notorious crime the following day.

In the warped reality he had created in his own mind, it would be a fitting revenge for the police visits to his mother's house while he had been a fugitive from the law.

He had already demonstrated that he was very accomplished indeed when it came to revenge – revenge for a 'disrespected' friend, revenge for an unpaid debt, even revenge for an attack that had not yet happened.

As part of a bitter feud between crime dynasties, he had murdered one of his rivals, Mark Short back in May, before killing his father, David, 12 weeks later.

Cregan had hated the Shorts since he was a schoolboy.

He had been involved in countless fist-fights and spats with them over the years and he jumped at the chance to murder the head of the family, the much-feared David Short.

But the assassination hadn't gone to plan.

David had been in the toilet when a masked Cregan opened fire in the Cotton Tree pub. Cregan still managed to shoot dead his son, Mark, and seriously hurt three other members of the Short family. Short snr sobbed as he cradled his dying son in his arms.

No matter.

Cregan finished the job soon after in a terrifying attack that first brought him to national prominence. He believed he had to murder Mark's grieving father to nip any attempt at revenge in the bud.

He had managed that with devastating aplomb and as the police continued to search the country for him, Cregan stalked the quiet suburban streets of Mottram in a bid to send the police his own terrifying and brutal message.

He wanted to indulge in one more ruthless ambush.

And this time, the target was the police themselves.

A KNOCK AT THE DOOR

Cregan chose very carefully and precisely where he was to slaughter police officers – any police officers.

Their names and rank weren't important. Nor how many.

His only wish was to murder someone, anyone, in a police uniform.

He chose a property right at the end of a quiet cul-de-sac – Abbey Gardens – to do the deed because he would be able to see the officers coming.

Later, the senior detective who investigated the murders would recall how similar tactics were adopted by the IRA in Northern Ireland.

He knocked on the door of a three-bed maisonette at around 10pm and invited himself in.

Cregan held three people hostage that night: local barber Alan Whitwell, his girlfriend Lisa McIntosh, and her young daughter, aged just seven.

Mother and daughter spent most of a terrifying night upstairs while Cregan enjoyed a party in the living room below.

It was Whitwell's misfortune that he knew Dale Cregan, although they weren't friends.

Despite the lack of a welcome or invitation, Cregan strolled across the hallway into the front room and held those inside hostage for the next 12 painful, desperate hours.

He was by turns charming and threatening.

A casual enquiry of 'how you been?' one second was followed by a clear threat the next: 'Do as I say or you will get hurt.'

During the evening that followed, Cregan threw himself a farewell party.

He knew this would be his last taste of freedom.

He drank beer, smoked cigars and surfed the internet, watching pornography and reading news stories about himself, the 'one-eyed fugitive'.

His captives endured a night of sheer terror, watching Cregan down successive beers and toy with and load his Glock semi-automatic pistol with its specially extended magazine in preparation for the murders which would follow.

"I heard a knock on the door," Whitwell would later recall.

"There was something different about it. It was strange. No-one knocks on a door at that time of night. I looked out of the window. I could see a shadow in the front garden. It was pretty dark outside. Although I couldn't see properly, I thought the figure looked familiar and I thought it was one of my mates. I shouted 'who's that?' and I heard a mumble. I'm sure they said 'it's Dale'. I thought it was a work colleague. I went downstairs and opened the door and standing there was Dale Cregan. I was in total shock. I knew immediately it was him because he only has one eye. His left eye is missing. I was really scared. I was just looking at his face. I was immediately petrified and feared for my life. I knew Dale Cregan was wanted by the police for murders.

"Dale Cregan was the last person I expected to see. He just walked straight in and said 'get in'. He was saying 'do as I say and if you don't, you will get hurt'. He walked into the kitchen and I closed the front door. He was talking to me as if I was his best mate saying things like 'how you been?'."

After he had casually strolled uninvited into the house, Cregan placed a hand grenade on the mantelpiece above the fireplace along with a bundle of cash.

No explanation was made. It wasn't necessary.

The grenade was an unspoken double threat. Firstly and obviously, it was a dangerous weapon of the kind he had used in a deadly attack just the month before.

And, secondly, there was the more subtle threat: Cregan had casually displayed it for everyone to see on the fireplace as a symbol of his power.

He knew his hostages could see it.

He wanted them to see it.

Cregan knew they were so scared of him they wouldn't go near it. There were also explicit threats to go with the implicit ones. "Do exactly as I say or I will shoot you," said Cregan, as he loaded 32 bullets into his modified handgun.

Whitwell described the fear that Cregan inspired: "There was no way I was going to ring the police because if they did turn up, who's to say he wasn't going to kill us first? I didn't care about the £50,000 reward. I'm not being funny. If somebody's got a gun and a grenade, I was going to do whatever they say. It was about my life and the lives of the others in the house. We tried not to panic and just to do whatever he says."

The hostage was ordered to 'fetch Garvs', a friend of Cregan's they both knew. He drove to Steven Garvey's house and told him: "Dale's at my gaff and he wants you to go now – we're going to have to go there now."

The vain hope was that Cregan would simply leave when Garvey turned up.

But the nightmare continued.

Cregan simply craved the company of familiar faces. There were forced pleasantries between the three men once Garvey had been collected.

Still, no-one mentioned the grenade which was perched on the mantelpiece. Cregan plundered some of the cash from the pile he had placed beside the grenade and ordered the two men to bring supplies for the farewell party he was about to throw himself.

They returned with bottles of Budweiser, cigarettes and cigars. The nervous chit-chat continued, with Cregan wavering about handing himself in.

"He was continually changing his mind about what he intended to do. He kept giving me false hope saying he was going to get off early and then saying he was staying through the night," said Whitwell.

As Cregan commandeered the house laptop, searching extensively for information about his beloved guns, he mocked the Shorts as 'muppets' and talked freely about how he had murdered his great rival, David Short.

Whitwell tried in vain to sleep. He managed just a few minutes. Proper sleep was impossible. During one nap, he was woken by Cregan shouting 'can I have your phone?' before making a series of random calls to people in the iPhone's contacts, some he didn't know. Cregan tried and failed to score cocaine.

The fugitive relaxed on the sofa and made a great show of playing with his Glock, clicking the mechanism backwards and forwards in front of his frightened audience.

A KNOCK AT THE DOOR

He had been 'chilling' while he had been on the run, he announced. He could have escaped abroad forever but he had wanted to stay in touch with his son, he insisted.

The beer finally took its toll and Cregan nodded off – briefly – on the sofa.

No-one dared make a run for it.

Sometime after 5am, Whitwell went upstairs where his girlfriend, Lisa, was still awake.

Her daughter, who Whitwell had tucked into bed before Cregan came knocking, was still sleeping.

"Try to be brave. Everything's going to be all right," he whispered, although he didn't believe his own words. He again tried to sleep but managed just a few more minutes before giving up and going downstairs.

He woke Cregan and – amazingly – told him he was off to work.

Cregan had ordered Whitwell not to veer from his normal routine and that meant heading to work as normal. But Whitwell couldn't concentrate. He texted Lisa, who was still cowering upstairs at home. 'I love you,' she texted back, confirming Cregan was snoozing again on the sofa.

It was too much for Whitwell who abandoned work and any pretence of normality and went back home.

"You're home early," Cregan said matter-of-factly when his hostage walked through the door, adding: "You're going to have to cut my hair. It needs a chop."

Whitwell got his clippers out and trimmed Cregan's beard, which had grown long and unruly while he had been on the run.

He had cut Cregan's hair before but his hands were trembling this time.

Cregan preened as his beard was sculpted just as he wanted.

He also popped in his most sinister looking prosthetic eye, made of black onyx, as he wanted to look at his most fearsome when he handed himself into police.

He also had a bath before changing into brand new clothes, ripping away the price tags before putting on a pair of shorts and a hoodie.

As the morning inched by, slowly and fearfully for Cregan's captives, he grew ever more restless as he prepared for his final and most terrible crime.

But, finally, he was ready.

Ready to launch an assault that would lead to shock, anger and uncomprehending sadness.

2.

FIONA AND NICOLA

September 18, 2012

Dawn was breaking on one of the darkest days in the history of British policing. It wasn't yet 7am and the police officers of C Relief, already in their uniforms, were driving through the early morning mist into the car park at Hyde Police Station in good time for the start of their shift.

Two of them, PCs Fiona Bone and Nicola Hughes, were not to know that each step they took was a step closer to their premature deaths.

The police station at Hyde is a modern and rather soulless building just outside the town centre, little more than a glorified bike shed like almost all new police buildings.

But the atmosphere inside the nick that morning was anything but sterile.

LIFE

One of the officers clocking on was 32-year-old PC Bone, who had been a bobby for five years. She was planning a civil partnership ceremony with her partner, Clare Curran.

They had booked time off to look for wedding dresses the following month. The pair lived together in Sale, a suburb about six miles south of Manchester, with Clare's young daughter, Jessie, from a previous relationship.

The plan was for Fiona to adopt Jessie – the beautiful little girl she adored and played with in the park as if she were her own. Only that morning the couple had chatted about invitations for the upcoming ceremony before Fiona slipped away from the house to go to work.

She pulled into the car park at 6.52am. Once she had walked into the station, the chatter was all about the new life she was about to begin with her partner. Just three minutes earlier, her other 'partner' pulled into the car park.

Fiona, a relatively experienced officer, would be paired with a fresh-faced and fearless rookie known as the station chatterbox, 23-year-old PC Nicola Hughes, from Diggle, near Oldham.

At Hyde, just six bobbies were tasked with answering 999 calls that day.

There weren't many of them, but they were Hyde's 'front line' in the fight against crime, and fiercely proud of it. The four other members of C Relief, one of the five shifts operated by Greater Manchester Police, arrived around the same time as PCs Bone and Hughes.

No matter that they were in the middle of a huge manhunt, the mood was happy. And Fiona was the main reason.

FIONA AND NICOLA

She had only recently announced she would be getting hitched. The hotel and photographer had been booked two days earlier. Now the invitations were being discussed.

Fiona showed them a draft she had designed herself and colleagues gave her tips about how to print them from a home computer to save money.

The two female officers were considered shining lights of the force, but for very different reasons.

Fiona symbolised the progress policing had made. She was proof that the force was inclusive, embracing anyone made of the right stuff regardless of their sexual orientation.

It wasn't all that long ago that gay officers felt obliged to keep their preferences secret.

Public spirit shone through – she volunteered with St John Ambulance; she set up a five-a-side team; she worked with a waterway restoration group.

Added to that, she was regarded as a bloody good copper.

She had been commended for her excellence in a burglary and robbery investigation, and she realised her job wasn't just about locking up the bad guys. It was typical of her 'everyone deserves a second chance' attitude that a man she had once arrested wrote her a letter of thanks for helping to turn his life around.

She impressed colleagues with her dedication, and her seniors with her extreme politeness.

On another occasion, when she had finished her shift, she felt so sorry for one victim of crime, she brought them a bunch of flowers.

And her abilities as a cop were all the better for the varied life she had experienced before she joined the police.

LIFE

She graduated from the University of Central Lancashire after a three-year Film and Media Studies degree. She had been captain of the women's rugby team while she was studying in Preston. Even though she was born in Norwich, she was a proud Scot, having been raised near Duffus, Scotland.

Later her father, Paul, an RAF aircraft engineer, moved the family to the Isle of Man after completing his career in the services at Castle Donington in Derbyshire.

After finishing her studies, Fiona moved to Manchester and worked for the insurance company Direct Line but found the work tedious in the extreme. The impulse to serve the public in some way was strong and she became a special constable before finally realising her dream by becoming a fully-fledged copper in 2007.

"She loved the job, she lapped it up. When she was put into an office, she hated it. She wanted to go where the action was," her father said.

And PC Bone had a big heart for someone so small.

She was a touch over 5ft 3in, so when there was a fence to be scaled in pursuit of a suspect, little Fiona would be the one to be thrown over it to continue the chase.

A job she loved, a partner she adored; Fiona was the happiest she had ever been.

* * *

Although she was still a rookie, Nicola was also admired, but for different reasons. It was the combination of toughness, bravery and compassion that set her apart. Like Fiona, Nicola was also sleight of frame, although at 5ft 6in tall, she could just about look down at her even smaller partner. Her courage belied her stature though.

She once climbed through a dog flap to enter a house and her colleagues had even thrown her over fences in the past as she pursued suspects.

On another occasion, she memorably waded into a pub brawl where the fists were flying to drag out an injured victim when still on probation.

The fact a mini-riot was going on in the middle of the boozer wasn't going to stop karate-mad Nicola doing her job.

With the help of a colleague, she dragged out the sozzled victim before he came to more harm.

Any experienced officer will tell you that no amount of training can properly prepare a probationer for the moment they come face to face with an 'angry man' for the first time.

Well, she was faced with several very angry and drunk men kicking lumps out of each other. The moment a fresh-faced copper truly finds out if they have the right stuff is the moment it happens for real.

It was clear that here was a proper bobby in the making.

Nicola's sergeant, who was standing outside the pub and watching her carefully, was impressed: "I checked Nicola's expression and there was no sign of fear."

She was taken to one side by her proud superior, who delivered a mock telling off to the young officer for going into the pub in the first place.

"It's over 21s only in there," said her smiling sergeant.

Fresh-faced Nicola, the wisp-of-a-thing who looked for all the world like a teenager who had somehow appropriated a police uniform for a laugh, must have swelled with pride.

It was as close to affirmation a young officer was going to get from her grizzled sergeant.

But it was enough.

The grizzled sergeant in question, Steve Miskell, came the nearest to summing up the little officer: "Friendly, full of life, always willing to give a helping hand, keen as mustard, as brave as they come and the chatterbox who always kept everybody else awake."

And Nicola was nothing if not a joyous bundle of contradictions. She might have been a karate expert, but she also liked hair dye and make-up.

She knew she had been accepted. When a night shift was dragging, Nicola would be the one keeping up everyone's spirits with her bubbly character and constant chatter. On patrol one day, she forced her bemused colleagues to stop the van so she could rescue a mouse being teased by two cats in the middle of the road. They were able to carry on with their duties, but only after Nicola had set the little mouse free in a nearby field.

Even when she was at Saddleworth School, her qualities stood out.

"She was the kind of person you could trust with your life," said her form tutor, Eddie Barton. And public service was in the family. Her father, Bryn, worked as a prison officer.

Out there on the streets, at all times of the day and night, when the rest of us are curled up in our beds, officers just like

FIONA AND NICOLA

PCs Bone and Hughes form the thin blue line, separating civilised society from the chaos and harm caused by criminals and ne'er-do-wells.

Most of the time we don't even notice them.

But they're there, doing extraordinary work so the rest of us can lead ordinary and peaceful lives.

Amid the happy chit-chat that filled Hyde Police Station that morning, however, there was serious business at hand.

The stand-in sergeant, Stuart Charlesworth, began the morning briefing at 7am sharp. He gave the six officers in front of him a round-up of what had happened overnight and allocated the first jobs of the day.

As is the modern practice, he delivered the briefing with a Powerpoint presentation, and at the top of his list of bullet points, as it had been for the previous six weeks, was the man who would kill Nicola and Fiona within a few hours.

Dale Cregan: The one-eyed killer. A man who had been the talk of Manchester – and especially its underworld – since he had shot dead Mark Short and then his father, David.

Dale Cregan: A man who had gone from nowhere to notoriety in the time it takes to murder two people.

They listened to the warnings they had heard dozens of times before – Cregan was a very dangerous individual; be extra vigilant; have your wits about you; if something doesn't look right, if an address you are visiting looks suspicious, call for back-up and don't go in.

They listened earnestly. They had become very familiar with Cregan and his startling police mugshot, complete with prosthetic eye. Extreme violence came very naturally to him, even from a very young age.

He had once smashed a bottle and rammed it up his victim's backside before twisting it, causing terrible internal injuries. In his youth he had been known as a 'local gobshite' by the beat bobbies who encountered him. He told the authorities he was a roofer.

Actually, he was a cocaine dealer, although his trade in narcotics would go undetected. He was clever enough to slip under the police radar and was not considered a major criminal figure, a 'no mark' in fact.

Cregan, like many of his contemporaries, was a gym monster, perhaps to make up for his lack of height. He was 5ft 10in.

He had become obsessed by weapons. He loved knives and had amassed an arsenal of guns, including semi-automatic guns. And, of course, he loved grenades – his 'pineapples' – as much for the fear they induced as the damage they caused.

Cregan revelled in his reputation as the first person to detonate grenades in Britain during peacetime.

With his array of weapons and love of extreme violence, he liked to take his victims by surprise and obliterate them with overwhelming force when they weren't ready.

His face was plastered all over the corridors of the police station, as it had been on the front pages of every newspaper in the land for weeks.

The two PCs left Hyde Police Station in a liveried VW Transporter at 7.56am. Their first job was to pick up a prisoner and take him to the cells at the North Manchester division headquarters at Central Park in Newton Heath.

They were back at Hyde station at 9.50am and ready for their next 'shout' of the morning. A line buzzed over at the police control room in Old Trafford at 10.16am.

It was a 999 call from Adam Gartree who reported he had seen someone throw a paving slab at the rear of his house.

The operator took the details and recorded the incident as an attempted burglary. Referring to the police call-handler as his 'mate', Gartree adopted a familiar tone during the three-minute call. When he briefly interrupted the flow of information to cough, the call-handler was moved to say: "It sounds like you've had a good night."

And, of course, he had.

The call-taker didn't know it but the man on the other end of the line was not a Mr Gartree.

It was Dale Cregan.

Cregan was clearly feeling the effects of his farewell party and the chummy-ness was an affectation, part of his ruse to lure police into his trap.

Eager to get on with his murderous plan, Cregan pushed the call-handler on how long it would take for officers to arrive at the house.

He was assured officers would arrive within the hour. The awful events which were about to unfold cast his response in a chilling light.

He signed off by saying: "Alright. Thanks very much. I'll be waiting."

After a pause, he repeated: "I'll be waiting."

One can only imagine his knowing, unseen smile at the other end of the line.

Again, the terrible sense of drama: he knew this was a phone call that would be recorded and would become public once the murders had been committed.

His three hostages were cowering upstairs and had no idea the call had been made.

As Cregan's call was coming to an end, another 999 came in. A man was kicking off at Hyde Job Centre and was refusing to leave.

As the more pressing incident, Cregan's report went to the back of the queue and PCs Bone and Hughes started to make their way to the job centre. By 10.27am they called back to say the man had now gone and an officer was no longer required. The two officers were stood down.

They could conceivably have continued their journey to the call-out to make sure everyone was okay, in which case they would still be alive today.

But the job was cancelled and the die was cast.

The bogus 999 call Cregan had made now jumped to the front of the queue and, at 10.36am, the two officers were ordered to head out to the address – Abbey Gardens in Mottram – some three miles away.

As it was not considered an emergency, they drove at normal speed along the M67 towards Mottram with Nicola at the wheel.

FIONA AND NICOLA

En route, Fiona got onto her radio and asked for any available intelligence on the address they were visiting. In normal circumstances, this would have been considered an unusual step.

But the request for vigilance in that morning's briefing, along with the repeated warnings about the danger Cregan posed over the previous weeks, was still ringing in the officers' ears. A check was made against the address and nothing untoward was revealed.

By 10.52am the two officers had arrived at Abbey Gardens.

Their VW Transporter turned left into the cul-de-sac and made its way slowly down the hill as the two officers scanned the houses on either side looking for the right number.

They were unaware Cregan was watching from behind a large window at the very end of the cul-de-sac, with a loaded 9mm Glock in one hand and a grenade in his jacket pocket.

His trap was nearly complete.

It was the perfect ambush.

He had chosen a house where he would be able to see his victims coming so he could prepare for the murders he would commit.

He had watched the van drive straight into one of five cobbled parking bays directly in front of the house.

The officers stepped out of the van, they negotiated a low wall, opened the garden gate and walked up to the front door.

PREVIOUS

3.

THE
SPARK

May 13, 2012

A day Manchester City fans will never forget.

It was also the day a simmering feud between two crime families reignited with spectacular and tragic consequences.

One argument, one measly incident in a pub, would eventually culminate in the brutal murders of four people: Mark Short, his father David and, as the summer came to an end, the terrible, tragic death of two innocent police officers.

And it could all be traced back to the giddy atmosphere in the Gardeners Arms pub on Edge Lane in Droylsden, which was packed with Manchester City supporters who were celebrating winning the top-flight title for the first time in 44 years.

It wasn't just the victory, but the manner of it.

All had seemed lost for Blues supporters as their home match against QPR went into injury-time.

They were losing 2-1 against a team with just 10 men. Worse, their arch rivals and illustrious neighbours Manchester United had won their match at Sunderland and were poised to lift the Premier League trophy yet again.

Dramatic injury-time goals, first from Bosnian Edin Dzeko and then Argentinian Sergio Aguero, turned heartbreaking defeat into unlikely victory for the long-suffering City supporters.

Cue delirium inside the Etihad Stadium, home of the Blues. The ecstasy inside the ground would continue for many, many weeks and months outside it, with City fans taking great pains to crow to their Red rivals about the victory made possible by the club's owner, Sheikh Mansour, who had ploughed an amazing £500m into a struggling team to secure the club's Premier League success.

Little wonder, then, that it was buzzing in the Gardeners Arms.

The big screens inside the pub had shown the game. Many supporters who had been at the match had come to the pub, just a mile and a half from the ground, to celebrate. All had travelled an emotional route familiar to any football supporter, from the depths of despair to unbridled joy.

One particularly giddy customer was Theresa Atkinson, matriarch of the notorious Atkinsons and a very happy City fan.

Not content with just celebrating victory, she was stirring things up.

THE SPARK

One of the other City supporters heading to the pub that night was David Short, a life-long Blue and the much-feared and violent head of another well-known crime family.

David Short had an unenviable criminal record.

He had form for drug dealing and violence. In 1988, then aged about 22, he was convicted of using threatening behaviour. He would add very many offences in the next few years: assault, GBH, drug dealing, even threatening witnesses who wanted to give evidence against him.

In 2006 he was convicted of possession of a firearm with intent to cause fear.

He was jailed for six years. He and his son Mark had driven a gunman away from a street after shots had been fired during daylight hours.

Six months after the shooting, Short snr battered a man during a drunken row at The Garibaldi pub in Gorton, leading to one of his convictions for GBH.

The Shorts would try their hand at any crime as long as it earned them a few quid.

They liked to conduct their business in the pubs around Clayton, which they considered their own turf. The terrified landlords dared not do anything about it.

In fact, such was the fear of reprisal, David had taken to wearing a bullet proof vest when he went about his illegal business.

In 2004 alone he was handed three official notices from the police warning him that his life was in danger.

He was urged to review his own security and move away from

the area. He certainly did the former but not the latter. A proud son of Clayton, there was no way he was moving away from Manchester because of an idle threat or two. He had grown up with such threats. They were part of his life by then. He was used to it.

Short's amateur boxer son Mark followed his father into a life of crime.

He was his father's son.

In fact, they were sometimes partners in crime. Short jnr admitted firearms offences following the shooting incident with his father in 2006.

Aged just 17, he was lucky avoid a stretch inside and was instead handed a community sentence. The warning he undoubtedly received from the judge – that he was at a crossroads and only he could decide whether he wanted to embark on a career as a criminal – was ignored.

By 2008, aged 19, he was sent down for five years and branded a dangerous young man by the sentencing judge after he had been convicted of robbery and GBH. Short jnr had been part of a gang of three who carjacked a 60-year-old man in Clayton. Three months later he knocked a shopkeeper unconscious.

For a man with no official earnings, David Short and his family lived well.

From the outside, his semi-detached house on Folkestone Road East looked like any other house in Clayton, one of Manchester's poorest areas. Inside, it was very well appointed. Downstairs, there was a purple and white decorated living room with two sofas and a large flatscreen TV mounted on the wall.

THE SPARK

The kitchen was brand new, decorated in blood red and white tiles. The property also boasted a large conservatory with another sofa. In the large back garden was a large trampoline where his grandchildren could play and at the end of the garden was a large outhouse with a gym inside, where he liked to keep himself fighting fit, literally. Upstairs there were three bedrooms.

So it was armed with a well-earned and fearsome reputation as one of Manchester's most dangerous criminals that David Short walked into the Gardeners Arms that day with his partner of 28 years, Michelle Kelly.

The pair bumped into Theresa Atkinson on their way in, and she put her arm around Short who, according to Michelle, had never met the woman before.

It was the beginning of an encounter between the two women that would bristle with aggression. Short went to the bar and Michelle headed over to the pool table. Theresa asked him if he wanted a drink, and he declined, saying: "I'm with my missus and my son."

Her reply was incendiary: "I'm not fucking asking them. I'm asking you."

Clearly affronted, Michelle Kelly stepped in: "You are being disrespectful and bang out of order... and with your attitude, he's not going to accept one." Michelle would later tell a jury: "I was angry with her and told her to get out of my way. Dave came over to say 'don't disrespect my missus'."

Theresa appeared to back down and apologised, buying Michelle a drink. But later she resumed her belligerent tone, calling David's amateur boxer son, Mark, a 'skinny little fucker' to his face. Short replied in kind about one of her sons, Charlie, who he said was a 'fat fucker'.

All these exchanges could have been passed off as merely colourful pub banter without the events that would unfold later.

And these were both fighting families who had been at loggerheads over one thing or another for more than 10 years.

Exactly when the bitter feud between the Atkinson and Short families began is difficult to pinpoint. The people at the heart of the dispute were never keen on chronicling their dispute.

But the shooting of Frankie Atkinson – Theresa's ex-husband – in 2003, was the earliest date the police uncovered in a search of their crime databases for incidents between the two families.

Was it the start of the feud? Almost certainly not. But it was as close to the genesis as police would get.

Back in 2003, Frankie Atkinson was enjoying a pint in The Victoria pub in Dukinfield when a masked man burst in.

The man behind the balaclava smashed Atkinson with the butt of a sawn-off shotgun, then opened fire.

By all accounts, Atkinson's knee was 'blown all over the pub' and he suffered a smashed jaw.

He spent a few weeks in a bad way in hospital and when he came out he was in a wheelchair for a while.

Replacement knee surgery would be required to allow him to walk freely again.

And although he was asked repeatedly who he thought was behind the mask that day, Frankie's lips remained sealed.

But he, along with the rest of his family, believed they knew who it was.

THE SPARK

For them, David Short was the masked gunman.

On May 7 of that same year – a Sunday night – another man allied to the Atkinsons was shot in another pub.

Career criminal Damian Gorman, who would later take part in the murder of Mark Short, was having a pint in the Old Dog in Denton. Details were sketchy but Gorman, then aged 27, was blasted in the chest and in the arm. He spent two months in hospital, much of it in intensive care and he had to have his spleen removed.

Despite his terrible injuries, Gorman was less than forthright with police when he was asked who had shot him in the pub. He didn't say who had done it, nor who he suspected might have done it.

But, again, the Short family were at the top of the suspects list.

The feud simmered for years until around 2009 when the two families decided to call an uneasy truce.

They met at the Arndale Centre in Manchester. At that meeting was David Short and Leon Atkinson, the son of Frankie and Theresa, and a man who had often butted heads – literally – with David Short.

The pair had been involved in numerous fist-fights down the years. Leon brought a friend to the meeting and Short brought along another member of the Short clan, John Short aka John Collins. The parties agreed that if there were problems in the future they would try to resolve them with a civilised conversation instead of a resorting to violence. Telephone numbers were exchanged. A handshake between old adversaries sealed the truce.

"We just said it's not worth fighting, shook hands and agreed to speak to each other on the phone if we had any problems," Leon Atkinson would later tell the trial.

The peace seemed to hold for a while.

But they were soon at it again.

The fighting resumed when Leon's brother, Jordan, was involved in a scrap with one of the Short clan and a member of Manchester's notorious Joyce family, who were broadly allied to the Shorts.

The phone numbers which had been exchanged during the peace talks at the Arndale were no longer needed.

It was open warfare again.

And that was the tense background to the increasingly heated exchanges in the Gardeners Arms as City fans drank heavily and shook their heads at the unbelievable Premier League success they had just achieved.

At around 8.30pm, and despite the mutual animosity, Theresa raised a few eyebrows when she decided to join the Short party when it left in taxis to head to another local boozer, the Cotton Tree Inn.

It was odd to say the least that Theresa wanted to join the Short party at the Cotton Tree, a regular haunt for the Shorts on Friday and Saturday nights. A friend Theresa had come out with had gone home and so – otherwise alone – she simply tagged along with the Shorts.

And she continued where she had left off in the Gardeners Arms.

"She was just being loud all the time... She was going around the pub talking to people and people were coming up to me and asking who she was. She was annoying everybody. I just told them to stay away from her," said Michelle.

It wasn't long before Atkinson was involved in a bust-up with another member of the extended Short family, Raymond Young.

Michelle Kelly explained: "I just heard shouting and arguing. At the time I didn't know what the argument was about. I just seen her run over to my table and grab an empty bottle of WKD and throw it at him."

The argument, according to Raymond Young, was about sexually suggestive comments Theresa had made, not to him, but to other young men in the pub, which had made him 'chuckle'. "She was saying stuff to the other lads which made me chuckle. That's why I got the crack," he said.

In her fury, she tried three times to bottle Young before he lashed out, slapping the older woman, aged 53, with the back of his hand.

He had been smashed in the face with a bottle. "I stood up, turned around and took the bottle off her. She grabbed another one and started swinging again. She went for another and that's when I gave her a back-hander. I pushed her towards the door," he said. "She was bladdered. I don't know who (she made the sexual reference) to but I found it funny, which is why I started chuckling. I was chuckling to myself and that's when I got whacked.

"When I pushed her towards the door, she came back in through another entrance and grabbed another bottle and someone else stopped her. I said 'who the fuck's that?' Someone said 'that's Theresa'.

"She goes and grabs another bottle off the table and goes to come after me again. Dave stopped her. He kept her over on that side of the pub. She was in there for a bit after it. She was going mad, going ballistic. She was saying 'you wait here – you're dead'. She was going round on the phone like a lunatic."

David Short and even his partner Michelle Kelly attempted to act as peacemakers but the increasingly menacing Theresa was having none of it.

"I'm going to get you done by my boys. I'm going to get you done by my sons. You just wait. You're dead," she said.

David Short was in no doubt that the execution of his son, who would die in his arms in the same pub 12 days later, had its roots in the spat with Theresa Atkinson, furious at being slapped by an upstart member of the Short's extended family.

"This is what I think it's all over," he would say to police.

Sozzled and humiliated, Theresa left the pub and started calling her sons, just as she had promised.

Police analysis of telephone bills showed the flurry of calls and texts between Theresa and her four offspring – Leon, Frankie jnr, Charlie and Jordan.

At 12.40am on May 14 she made the first of many calls, to Leon.

Known as Acky, Leon made a passable impression of a legitimate, hard-working businessman. He was involved in property development and also worked as a gas fitter.

He took a 61-second phone call from his mother that night and the sequence of calls and texts, including to her ex-husband

Frankie, would continue for a couple of hours, until just after 3am.

Theresa and Leon slept on the incident but more texts were exchanged and they spoke again at 8.09am.

There was no doubt that Theresa was still fuming after what had happened the night before.

And one close friend of the Atkinsons happened to be a certain Dale Cregan.

Cregan and Leon Atkinson were both regulars at a gym in Stalybridge, Ultimate Fitness, and Leon sent Cregan a text at 8.46am before Cregan called back at 8.59am.

Only they know what was said during their call, which lasted two minutes and seven seconds, and in the subsequent trial that followed, the prosecution could not prove beyond doubt that Leon had asked Cregan to seek revenge on the Short family.

In fact, Cregan had long hated the family himself and had more than enough reasons to go after them.

Cregan's upbringing had been overshadowed by the Shorts, who often travelled to Droylsden from their patch in Clayton to muscle in on the action and try and beat up Cregan and his friends.

The Shorts saw Droylsden as theirs for the taking and Cregan had grown to massively resent their belligerent influence.

Their shared history therefore meant Cregan was more than happy to go after the Shorts.

However, he also knew that his formidable enemies could cause him serious harm. He did not want to take those risks alone and he decided he needed sub-contractors.

First he called a friend and fellow Ultimate Fitness member, Luke Livesey – a wheeler-dealer he had known for eight years – to be his henchman.

Then he called and recruited his driver, Damian Gorman. Gorman, a nasty piece of work who revelled in the nickname 'Scarface', was in Spain when he took the call but it didn't stop him joining the team of assassins.

Eventually, Preston Crown Court would hear that Cregan also recruited Ryan Hadfield – his best mate – and also Matty James to act as spotters in the pub but the duo – along with Leon Atkinson – were later found not guilty of murdering Mark Short.

A few days after Theresa had been slapped in the pub, the Atkinsons despatched a go-between to the home of David Short in Clayton, east Manchester.

Leon had sent him to get a mobile number for the head of the Short clan. David wasn't prepared to give it, but he would call Leon.

During the subsequent conversation, Leon was clear – his mum had come home with bruises on her face and she blamed Raymond Young.

David Short was equally clear – she had been 'out of order' and insisted the slap could not have been strong enough to bruise her. Leon suggested he and Raymond have 'a meet', in other words a fist-fight, to settle matters.

When the offer was declined, Leon suggested Raymond fight one of his brothers. That too was turned down.

Raymond told Leon straight, that there would be no fight because he was a 'dodgy cunt'. Raymond recalled the conversation: "He was calm. He didn't raise his voice. He said it shouldn't have happened. But it was her who started on me and that's why I gave her a slap. That was it. No problem. As soon as I put the phone down, Dave was saying 'take whatever they say with a pinch of salt'."

Leon was embarrassed at his 'bladdered' mum mouthing off, agreeing she had been 'clipped' but only as Young tried to protect himself. David Short offered to send some flowers and chocolates to Theresa to draw a line under the saga. Leon declined as it was 'not necessary'.

The problem appeared to be over. But Cregan had other ideas. His plan was taking shape.

All he needed was the right time and the right place.

4.

THE COTTON TREE

May 25, 2012

The Short family believed it was just another Friday night when they headed out, first to the Gardeners Arms and later onto the Cotton Tree as had become their habit.

It had been a hot day with temperatures reaching 25 degrees Celsius in Manchester. Most of the revellers in the Cotton Tree that night were wearing shorts and t-shirts. The Shorts were simply enjoying a night out and were completely unaware of the plot that was unfolding behind their backs.

The plan had been set. Cregan would carry out the shooting with the help of fellow cocaine dealer Damian Gorman who would drive the getaway car while Luke Livesey would be a passenger.

Earlier in the evening, Cregan and Livesey went to The Organ pub where they met their driver, Gorman.

To onlookers, Cregan appeared not to have a care in the world as he sat in the beer garden, wearing flip-flops, shorts and a vest.

After a few beers, Cregan and Livesey headed to Glossop to pick up the stolen Ford Focus which would be used to take the assassins to and from the Cotton Tree for the hit.

It was on.

Unconfirmed reports suggest Cregan and his team did a practice run, even leaning out of the car during the drive-by and shouting 'you're dead' to members of the Short party, some of whom were out on the pavement.

Police were never able to confirm it but detectives were able to establish that the Focus drove past the pub about 11 minutes before the hit.

Nothing was said. No-one leaned out of a window to make a threat. It was a recce. Last orders was called at 11.45pm and just a few minutes later, the Ford Focus drove up to the pub a second time.

It was parked up beside the entrance with its hazard lights on.

CCTV from the other side of Market Street captured a dark figure getting out of the car and walking briskly into the pub.

It was Dale Cregan.

He walked through a side door closest to where the Short party members were playing pool and darts. Through the eye-holes of his balaclava, he saw the targets and opened fire.

He loosed off seven shots and calmly walked out again. He jumped back into the car and sped away.

THE COTTON TREE

The hit had taken just 24 seconds from the moment the car pulled up to the moment it sped away.

His shooting spree had caused carnage in the pub.

David Short's son, Mark, lay dying in his father's arms. Three others were also hit. Witnesses described how the gunman appeared to be carefully choosing his targets before shooting them.

Cregan would later express only two regrets – that he had not been able to get hold of a hand grenade that day and that his real target, David, who fortuitously had gone to the toilet, had evaded him.

Cregan carefully picked out Mark and blasted him three times, once in the neck.

Short snr, saw a scene of utter bedlam when he came back from the toilet. His son died there beside the pool table as his sobbing father tried to comfort him.

Three others were seriously hurt, Mark's cousins, John Collins and Michael Belcher, and Belcher's uncle, Ryan Pridding.

Recalling events later in court, grieving mother Michelle Kelly, said: "I heard one bang and I turned around and then I seen him. My son had his back to me.

"And then the second one went off. Then it was just bang, bang, bang." Her son, who had been standing right beside his killer, had tried in vain to grab the gunman, she told the court. She even grabbed a pool cue and ran out of the pub after the gunman – but all she saw was the getaway car speeding off.

"Mark had never done nothing wrong," she told the jury. "He was playing a game of pool and he got shot... At the end of the day my son was brutally murdered. I had to sit there and see my husband sob like a baby because he had seen his son murdered."

After the slaying of Mark, David Short pointed the finger of blame at the apparent humiliation of Theresa Atkinson but – according to his partner – he had resisted the temptation to take the law into his own hands.

Police intelligence suggested otherwise, that David Short was bent on revenge.

They believed he had made it known around east Manchester that he would kill Dale Cregan and the rumour was that he would rape and kill Cregan's sister and son.

It may well have been a case of 'an eye for an eye' as far as Short was concerned.

About a week after his son's death, David Short gave a statement to the police about the murder. The atmosphere in the pub had been 'really good'. He was surrounded by his family.

He recalled: "I had been there a few hours playing pool against Mark and I decided to go to the toilet. When I came out of the toilet, I heard bang, bang, bang. Instantly, I thought it sounded like a gun and I went back into the toilet. When I came out I saw John (Collins) on the floor. I just remember someone telling me 'Mark's been shot'. I looked down and I saw him on the floor. At first I couldn't believe it. I went over to Mark and put my hand under his head and started talking to him. I could see he was dying. He was lifeless."

Ryan Pridding, who had been shot in the thigh and knee, said: "Everyone was shouting and screaming. I crawled over to John (Collins) and asked if he was okay. I heard Raymond shout

'Mark's in a bad way'. I saw Mark was hit. Dave had hold of him, crying, saying 'please, please, son, please Mark'. I heard Michelle screaming 'what am I going to do Dave? What am I going to do?'

Michael Belcher didn't realise he had been shot in the leg at first. He said: "I thought someone was messing about, kicking me in the leg. I didn't realise until someone started shooting. I started to crawl towards the toilet and the gunshots were still happening. I tried to get out through the back door."

Raymond Young was also in the pub but miraculously escaped unhurt.

One of the seven shots which had been fired passed through the front of the shorts he had been wearing that night.

He joked that his lucky escape was down to 'skinny legs'.

He tried to stem the bleeding from a gunshot wound to the back of his cousin John Collins. He also tried to help Mark Short, lifting up his top to expose the neck wound and tried in vain to stop the bleeding from his severed carotid artery.

John Collins, another east Manchester hard man, was blasted in the back as he was throwing a dart and collapsed to the floor.

He told the court he thought the 'problems with the Atkinsons had been squashed a few years ago', although he admitted it had been 'tit for tat' before an uneasy peace had broken out.

The Short name, he told police, had been a 'curse', and he was glad to have taken his mother's name instead of Short.

The feud between the families had been directed 'all towards Dave', although he was 'not a bad man'.

"He's not very well liked," said Collins, "but then I'm not very well liked either. A lot of people are disappointed I'm not dead and even more disappointed they didn't get Dave. But they did didn't they? Someone did... I'm no angel but I have got morals."

He believed Short snr had been the target: "I didn't think I was the target. I was a bonus."

The feud between the families had started when Collins was a 'young lad', but he thought Short snr had borne the brunt of it: "It wasn't that long ago he had his throat cut."

Collins, like Michelle Kelly, insisted that David Short had not acted on any vengeful thoughts he may have had. He told the jury: "No. Did he do anything? Did the police arrest him for anything? They told him to stay out of it and that's what he did. He didn't do anything."

Pointedly looking over at Cregan in the dock, he continued: "He didn't kidnap anyone. He didn't kick any doors in. He went to the police and said let them do their job. And what a mistake! He didn't even know who had done it. How can he (take) revenge on someone? Chinese whispers never really add up to much do they?"

One witness who was in the pub at the time of the shooting described the terrifying moment she came face-to-face with the gunman.

Chelsea Evans said: "The side door to the pub always squeaks when it opens. I heard a squeak and looked up... I looked at him. They were dressed all in black and wore a black balaclava... They stood half in and half out of the door. I didn't really pay much attention to the object in his hand. I just remember thinking 'please don't let that be what I think it is'. I saw this person fire what I believe to be a gun. The person's arm was outstretched in the direction of Mark Short, who was close by. I think the person with the gun was aiming at Mark's head as they held the gun quite high. I heard a noise and saw sparks and saw Mark fall to the floor. To me it looked like they were aiming at whoever they intended to shoot... I didn't believe it had actually happened. I felt I was going to have a heart attack. I was physically sick. I was in shock. I have never felt as bad in my entire life."

A police officer, PC Phillip Pilkington, had been escorting a drunk prisoner back to the station when he was flagged down.

He ran into the pub and tried chest compressions while a colleague attempted mouth-to-mouth resuscitation.

It was no use.

The first paramedic who arrived at the scene told the officers to step aside and he could see there were no signs of life. Mark Short was pronounced dead at the scene.

The assassins were long gone. They had taken the back roads towards Hollingworth to torch the car and burn incriminating evidence.

They set fire to the car and CCTV would capture them rather bizarrely walking single file and separated by a metre all the way as they trekked for the half mile to the 'clean up' property at Moorfield Terrace, which was empty.

Getaway driver Gorman knew it well as he had only moved out of it a few months earlier.

But the gang had made a big mistake.

For some reason they didn't burn the clothing they had worn during the hit once they arrived at the house in Hollingworth. Maybe the sound of the fire brigade arriving to put out their burning Ford Focus on the other side of the village had spooked them. The smell of detergent on the clothes suggested they had tried to wash away any incriminating evidence, but to no avail.

The forensic testing of the clothing, the results of which came back some three months after the murder, would be enough to persuade the CPS to charge Cregan and the others.

Two days after the shooting, Leon Atkinson was lifted by the police as he was driving his Vauxhall van through Swinton in the borough of Salford.

He knew he would be arrested at some point and he had his story straight.

The wags on Facebook – allies of the Shorts who had taken to the internet to point the finger of blame at the Atkinson family – had got it wrong. He told the officer: "I was expecting this because I've heard people have been talking shite."

Arrested on suspicion of murder, he made no comment during six hours of police interviews. He did, however, provide a measured, prepared statement through his solicitor. Detectives at first, wrongly, suggested he had taken part in the shooting itself, but Atkinson had an alibi.

At the moment Mark Short was being blasted to death, Leon was with his girlfriend and their two daughters, aged four years and five months, at his business partner's large four-birth caravan at Prestatyn Sands in North Wales.

THE COTTON TREE

His mother, Theresa, would join them later.

Leon Atkinson went on a trip to the seaside at Rhyl, and had breakfast at Liffey's Cafe where he enjoyed scrambled eggs and salmon on brown bread toast. He bought a tuna mayonnaise sandwich which he would eat later for his lunch. He went shopping and bought a swimsuit for one of his children.

The Atkinson party returned to Prestatyn Sands and watched their kids on the playground. Leon kept the receipts from his trip to north Wales, which meant he could categorically prove he was elsewhere.

Each verifiable detail deflated the police case, which remained largely in the dark at that early stage of the murder investigation.

Atkinson told a story about a strange man who he had seen at the caravan site who had jumped over a fence and driven away in a car when he was challenged.

He suggested later that maybe the Shorts had sent someone to follow his mother. So the caravan break was abruptly cut short and Leon decided he, his girlfriend, their two children, his mother and a child by a late former partner would drive back to Manchester in his Audi, with his mother following in convoy, because of 'concern for the safety' of his family.

Explaining away the 'shite' he had referred to on his arrest, Leon said in his prepared statement that 'information had been circulating on Facebook which suggested my family were somehow responsible for the incident on Friday night'. He added: "I was not in the Cotton Tree pub on May 25, 2012. I was in North Wales. The last time I was in that pub was at least two years ago. I'm not responsible for this incident and I have no knowledge of it."

He was released on bail and when he returned to a police station with his solicitor, he declared himself 'pleased' that his alibi had been checked and verified.

However, that did not stop police from making further investigations before finally charging him with the murder of Mark Short and the attempted murders of three others in the Cotton Tree.

Meanwhile, Cregan celebrated what he thought was a textbook hit with a lads' holiday.

A week after the assassination of Mark Short, he flew business class to the Peace Resort on the idyllic island of Koh Samui, Thailand. He spent 10 days relaxing there with Luke Livesey, best friend Ryan Hadfield, and three other pals.

It wasn't Cregan's first time in Thailand.

He had been many times. It was during one of these previous visits he lost his left eye in a scrap when he apparently picked on the wrong Thai.

The story was that his face had been smashed in with a spiked knuckle-duster. A little embarrassed, Cregan returned home, had his eye removed, and told his pals that it had been lost in a scrap with Thai police in a bid to bolster his hardman image.

Other rumours suggested that Cregan had actually lost the eye when it was removed under torture.

Either way, it added a gruesome extra dimension to his image as he began wearing a prosthetic eye to replace the plucked out eyeball.

When Cregan returned from his holiday, the police were waiting.

THE COTTON TREE

He was arrested on June 12 after stepping off the flight from Thailand before being released on bail pending the outcome of further enquiries.

Cregan believed he had to lie low in case the Shorts launched a revenge attack for the killing of Mark.

After months of staying quiet, Cregan finally decided to leave the area for a hotel in Bowness, overlooking Lake Windermere, alongside his mum Anita, girlfriend Georgia Merriman and their son.

They arrived in the Lake District on August 6, 2012, just four days before he committed the murder of David Short. Flush with drugs money and keen to get away from the Shorts, Cregan was thinking about moving to the Lakes permanently and he checked out rental properties.

However, the tranquility of escaping Manchester was shattered the next morning when Cregan found out that police were looking for him and wanted to arrest him again over the murder of Mark Short.

He had originally been told that he had to return to a police station on August 14, the following week.

But detectives couldn't wait until then.

Forensic tests had been done in between Cregan's bail and that date in August, and they now had the results.

Police had compelling DNA and gunshot residue evidence that implicated Cregan in the murder of Mark Short.

So they decided to arrest Cregan and others on August 7 and charge them with murder.

They managed to find and arrest his mates Livesey, Gorman

and Hadfield that morning but Cregan was proving elusive.

It didn't take long for him to find out about the news over in Manchester and realise he was a wanted man.

The restful break beside the calm waters of Windermere was over. It was time to return to Manchester and finish the job; finish David Short.

The grief-stricken father had buried his son at Droylsden cemetery within a few days of the murder, and visited Mark's graveside like clockwork three times every day, in the morning, at noon and then in the evening.

It had become a tragic routine.

Cregan considered him 'unfinished business'. Perhaps fearful of the revenge that never happened, Cregan decided he should get his revenge in first.

With his twisted sense of drama, he began to formulate a plan to murder David Short.

And he would try and kill him while he grieved at his son's graveside.

5.

UNFINISHED BUSINESS

August 10, 2012

For the first time in the three months since his son's murder, David Short decided against visiting the grave of his son Mark.

Instead, he ran an errand. When he returned to his home in Clayton, he was unaware he was being watched.

Crouching low beside the next-door neighbour's garden gate was Cregan, wearing shades and checking out his unsuspecting target.

The assassin knew that Short visited his son's graveside three times a day at Droylsden Cemetery.

For an hour, he had been watching and waiting at the cemetery, but the target never turned up.

Cregan had to change his plan – instead of murdering Short as he wept over Mark, he would kill him at his home.

He went to the house in a hired van with two accomplices, Anthony Wilkinson and Jermaine Ward.

As they watched on, Short lifted the boot of his Renault Megane and carried new chrome furniture into his house.

Of course, he was never going to forget how he had sobbed and cradled his own son as he died of gunshot wounds in the Cotton Tree just weeks before. Nevertheless, his mood had lightened.

He exchanged pleasantries with a neighbour and mentioned a kids' barbecue later in the day. His daughter Stacey and three grandchildren would no doubt have been guests. It was a lovely, sunny morning.

Wearing just shorts and trainers and laden down with another piece of furniture, he walked bare-chested into his home, leaving the front door open.

Unseen, Cregan gave the nod to Wilkinson.

With his Cotton Tree assassins banged up and awaiting trial, Cregan had had to look further afield to find murderous allies in his bid to kill David Short.

Cregan eventually turned to Wilkinson, a 6ft 2in hardman from Beswick in Manchester. Cregan could rely on 'Wilko' to be loyal and knew Wilkinson could handle a gun.

In fact, Wilkinson considered himself Cregan's equal rather than an employee when it came to crime.

Aside from helping his friend Cregan, Wilkinson knew the murder of David Short would solve a few personal problems. Wilkinson owed Short £20,000, so removing him from the scene would save a lot of headaches.

UNFINISHED BUSINESS

Wilkinson was ready and armed as Cregan beckoned his friend over.

Chaos was about to reign.

The pair calmly walked across the flagstones up to the open front door and opened fire on Short, who was taken completely by surprise.

Cregan used his favoured Glock semi-automatic pistol.

It was carnage, as brutal a slaying as can be imagined.

The trail of his blood showed Short was chased through the living room, into the kitchen and conservatory and then out through the garden until he was finally trapped behind a gate in an alleyway beside the house, where more shots were fired down onto him after he had collapsed to the ground.

It was a cold-blooded execution.

Most of the shots Short took had been to the front of his body. It was clear he had seen his attackers and was backing away from them through the house.

Only Cregan and Wilkinson know what, if anything, was said as they gunned him down. Perhaps mention was made of the perceived sleight on Theresa Atkinson, slapped all those months earlier by Raymond Young.

Perhaps David Short was mocked as he was repeatedly blasted for having failed to take revenge over his son's death.

Perhaps Cregan was thinking about his own son, who he had arranged to be taken somewhere safe moments after the murder.

As he lay dying from terrible gunshot injuries, a grenade was tossed into the alleyway.

Short was probably spared the terror of seeing it rolling beside him with its pin removed. It is highly unlikely he was conscious when the device landed beside him in the alleyway.

If what was said during the attack can only be guessed at, there were a number incontrovertible facts about the assassination: David Short was shot 10 times, twice to the head, and was already dying when Cregan lobbed the grenade beside his already injured body.

When it detonated, it devastated his body further and caused a crater in the ground and split a nearby gas pipe. Some of his internal organs were destroyed beyond recognition.

Pieces of his flesh were found all over the alleyway and at the front of his house.

Cregan's only regret was that he had not fetched a knife from the kitchen so he could chop off his victim's limbs and head.

"I shot David Short point-blank in the head, three times, but I would have preferred it if I would've used a knife. I felt calm before killing David Short but, after, a big relief rushed through my body. If I had time, I would have cut his head off. I would have cut his legs and arms off. I would have gone and got a knife from the kitchen and used that. The thoughts were such, I knew I would have to do it," Cregan would later tell a psychologist and a psychiatrist.

Cregan and Wilkinson ran into a waiting van, where a third man – their getaway driver, Jermaine Ward – was waiting to speed them away.

Ward, like Wilkinson, was also a friend of Cregan's who knew him from the drugs business. On the day he took part in the murder of Short, he had been due in court to be sentenced over a £360,000 amphetamine supply racket.

After the slaughter, the trio were evidently pleased with their work. A neighbour overheard one of them, probably Cregan, saying 'that one did it'.

Inside the van, Cregan had Short's blood on his face and shirt. Yet it was a moment of celebration. He and Wilkinson bumped fists and laughed.

The detonation at Folkestone Road East was an unwanted landmark in British criminal history.

August 10, 2012, marked the first time anyone had used a hand grenade in anger in Britain during peacetime.

A Home Office pathologist, Dr Phillip Lumb, had the unenviable task of examining what remained of the body of David Short. The 11 major sites of injury he found suggested the victim had been hurt in a warzone rather than murdered as part of a feud between two local families.

A scan of the body revealed five bullets and countless tiny grenade pellets, just two millimetres in diametre, lodged in his frame. One of the bullets had passed through the top of his head, fracturing his skull and damaging his brain before exiting near his cheek.

Another went in near to his mouth and severed a major artery before coming to rest in his neck. A third bullet hit just to the side of his jaw, went through his brain and exited at the top of his head. Other bullets struck his arm, torso, left thigh and grazed his neck. A large area of his back and left side was obliterated by the grenade explosion.

Many of his internal organs were barely recognisable, according to Dr Lumb, who surprised no-one when he concluded the death was caused by 'multiple gunshot wounds and a grenade explosion'.

He made other observations of note: some of the injuries may well have been 'defensive', for instance the bullet wound to his left hand; and the grenade hastened a death that was already certain.

"Although he was dying, I think he was still alive when the grenade detonated. It very likely accelerated his death," was how Dr Lumb put it.

Inside the home, there were clear signs of how domestic calm had suddenly been shattered.

Short's keys and cash were found on one of the lounge sofas.

In the kitchen, freshly made toast had sprung up in the toaster.

The ironing board had been knocked to the floor in the kitchen. Shattered glass from a table was strewn across the back garden. A garden chair had been up-ended. The aftermath of David Short's desperate struggle to save his own life was clear to see for the police. The grenade explosion was enough to sever a gas pipe as well as ensure a man's death.

Later, scores of households had to be evacuated while the hissing gas pipe was made safe. Aside from the risk to life and limb, police were concerned any subsequent explosion could destroy key evidence.

Army bomb disposal officers would comb the area for more explosives. Householders would only be allowed back into their properties before nightfall, about 12 hours after the murder.

Terrified neighbours who cowered in their homes described hearing an 'almighty bang'.

Peter Tague said: "There was a bang and then another bang. I thought 'shit, it's kicking off' and I rang 999... The kitchen shook when the first bang took place."

His wife, Christine Tague, had just waved her father away in his car when she saw a man – Cregan – kneeling down at a gate at the house next door to David Short's. She said he wore sunglasses and looked as if he was painting the gate. She mistook the coat he had placed on the pavement as a decorator's sheet. Mrs Tague, who had been watching the Olympics on TV, described how she was putting shopping away in the kitchen when she heard a loud bang. She recalled: "It sounded very loud. It was just so loud. It's something you don't expect. We knew it was a shotgun because it was so loud. And then there were more shots, we counted about nine."

Mrs Tague described how she shut the blinds and heard another 'louder' bang, which was the grenade going off. "We heard like an explosion. It was very different. It was just a terrifying, almighty bang. You can't put it into words. It was so loud. We thought there had been an explosion or something. It was just so loud," she said. She described how her husband called the police and how they only went outside after hearing the noise of neighbours chatting outside. "We were just so shook up, frightened and traumatised by it," she said.

One of the first police officers on the scene was PC Trevor Williams, part of an armed unit.

Alerted to a possible shooting, he arrived to see a crowd of people who had gathered around the Short house, and they directed him into the property.

As he made his way to the house, the officer noticed blood and pieces of flesh on the ground. He found the body of Mr Short behind the gate and immediately called for more assistance on his radio.

His colleague PC Peter Shrimpton saw blood and spent bullet casings on the ground as he ran to the house. "I could see a body in the alley which was clearly deceased. It had multiple severe injuries including a massive head wound. I could see a blood trail leading around the corner of the house," said PC Shrimpton.

Paramedic Christopher Wheeler was called to the scene but was ordered to remain at a nearby Asda store until police had ensured the area was safe.

When he got there, he also noted the blood and human tissue on the ground, something he admitted he had never seen before. He opened the side gate and saw Short on the floor. "As soon as I saw him I knew straight away he was dead," said the paramedic.

Cregan and his henchmen had gone but they weren't finished.

Just nine minutes after the attack which claimed David Short's life, they carried out another savage assault.

CCTV captured Cregan and Wilkinson outside a house on Luke Road in Droylsden.

Inside, Sharon Hark was home alone and about to have a shower when she heard a noise. Cregan tried to fire his gun at the property. When it misfired he simply took out a second gun and used that. Then he tossed a grenade, which detonated in the small front garden, shattering a front window.

UNFINISHED BUSINESS

Ball bearings from the grenade were propelled in all directions, even piercing a conservatory door of a neighbouring property.

It was only a matter of fortune that no-one was killed, let alone injured.

Mrs Hark would later tell police she was baffled why the semi-detached home she had shared with her husband Robert for the previous 26 years had been attacked in that way.

Yes, her son Jason had been involved in a fight with someone two years earlier, but grenades and guns? This was "out of his league," she declared.

Police believe the attack may have been down to a debt her son apparently owed to Cregan.

Mrs Hark had been in Manchester when the IRA detonated a bomb in 1996. The noise she heard sounded just like that. She explained to police how her mundane domestic concerns were shockingly interrupted: "I woke at 9.15am and went to the living room at the front of the house. I didn't feel well. I had been unwell since the previous day. I took two paracetamol and had a cup of tea. While I was on the phone, Robert said he was popping out. I don't know where he was going.

"Before he went, he asked me to put the washing out, which I did. I put it out in the rear garden and decided to wash my hair and walked into the bathroom, which is downstairs. I had my back to the window at the front of the house. The blinds were almost closed. I was about to turn the shower on when I heard a loud bang I cannot describe. It sounded like a large explosion had occurred. At this stage I didn't think anything was wrong but I was baffled by the sound. I could tell the explosion had come from the front of the house. I heard one big bang that lasted about a second. I remember it reminded me of the sound I heard when the Arndale Centre was bombed in the 1990s. I went into the living room and looked out of the blinds and I could see three panes of glass had been shattered. People had gathered out on the street outside. I went to open the front door and as I did I saw the porch window had been shattered. I just wanted to get back in my house. I was on my own and shocked by what had happened. My husband was still out of the house and my son was on his way back from Liverpool where he lives with his girlfriend."

She said she was at a loss to explain why her home would be attacked: "Whilst (Jason) stays at my house and still socialises with people from the Droylsden area, if he goes out at all he will go and see his sister who lives near. My family does not have enemies.

"Jason had a fight with a local boy about two years ago. The boy he had been fighting with put our windows through. He went to court for that although he didn't get a prison sentence. He received a fine. What happened at my house was out of his league."

Mrs Hark said when she went to work the following day, younger colleagues were chatting about what had happened. "I tend not to listen to people gossiping because it's just that – gossip," she said.

In a subsequent police interview, Mrs Hark told officers her daughter had gone to the same school as Cregan. Mrs Hark said: "I'm aware of Dale Cregan and seen his photo in the news, but if he passed me in the street, I wouldn't know him.

UNFINISHED BUSINESS

"As far as I'm aware, he's never been in our house or socialised with anybody in our family. I have absolutely no idea why this has happened to my home or my family, or why my family has been targeted."

6.

WHITE HEAT

With smoke billowing from the explosion at Luke Road, Cregan fled again with Wilkinson and the getaway driver, Ward, after detonating his second grenade in nine minutes.

Except this time they abandoned the Salford Van Hire Vauxhall Combo van parked just down the road which had taken them to both crime scenes. Cregan tossed a third grenade into the back of the van, intending it should destroy any evidence linking him or his colleagues to the crimes.

The detonation blew out the sides of the van and punctured the body work. The blast was so powerful it shattered the rear window of a car parked 50 metres away. Led by the getaway driver, Ward, who was carrying Cregan's heavy bag of munitions, the three assassins went on foot across the nearby Lees Park to their second getaway car, a Ford Fiesta Cregan had bought under a false name for cash the previous day and parked up in readiness for the escape.

As the trio fled, the householders around Luke Road were wondering what on earth was going on.

Shirley Holmes and her husband Derek were in their hallway when they heard a bang. Shirley would later tell the police: "My instant reaction was to go into the kitchen as I believed my washing machine or cooker had exploded. When I saw they were still in tact we went to go outside to check if the explosion was from one of the neighbours' house.

"We were both still indoors when there was a second very loud explosion which blew a panel off our side gate. We both came back into the house and walked into the lounge and looked out of the window and saw parked on a pathway outside a small Salford Van Hire van with the rear doors open and the driver's door window also open. I saw two figures disappearing over a grass embankment heading in the general direction of Oldham Street. They were facing each other as though they were in conversation. One appeared to be wearing a baseball cap.

"Once the two figures disappeared, I went outside and could see the windscreen and driver's window of the van had been smashed, and then I realised the explosion had come from the van. I went back into the house and then looked outside and heard shouting coming from the street and saw two police officers outside with guns. I told them I had seen two figures going across Lees Park. They told everybody to stay indoors."

Cregan, Wilkinson and Ward rushed across the park, got into the Fiesta and headed north to Failsworth.

By now police were swarming all over east Manchester and Tameside. Police Armed Response Vehicles, usually Range Rovers, were at Folkestone Road East. Some were diverted to Luke Road.

One of the diverted armed police officers was PC Gareth Davies, who got out of his unmarked police car and pursued the three men across the park. Public-spirited residents told him they'd seen two men responsible for the shooting head across the park and he headed that way with his weapons ready.

He described running over small ball bearings in the road. He saw tiny holes in the Vauxhall Combo van. He got onto the radio and alerted the police control room to the possibility that grenades had been used in the attack.

The police were getting close. Their airwaves were a confusion of information, some of it relevant but most of it not.

Clarity and certitude tend to evaporate in the white heat which characterises the first hour of any major police investigation.

Reports were coming in of a silver-coloured Ford Fiesta car being spotted in Failsworth.

Just after 11.30am, PC Colin Whalley thought he was onto something.

By now he and every officer in Greater Manchester Police was aware of the murder in Clayton and the attack nine minutes later in Droylsden.

And more than likely they knew the dead man was the father of Mark Short, gunned down three months earlier. The bobby was on a routine patrol on Ashton Road West in Failsworth, and he was looking for the Fiesta.

Near Tesco, he spotted two suspicious characters.

And they spotted him.

One of them looked down to avoid looking at the officer, who was about to turn his patrol car round when he spotted a parked Fiesta.

Then one of the men bolted towards some shops. PC Whalley gave chase on foot. He looked around the shops but his man was nowhere to be seen. Moments later, he saw the man climb over a fence into some overgrown fields.

The officer vaulted metal railings to chase him down. He lost sight of the man but moments later saw him again running across a car park. PC Whalley resumed his chase only to be thwarted by a large van which pulled into the car park, blocking his view.

The suspect was out of sight and gone. By radio, he was ordered to abandon the chase and the force helicopter, India 99, resumed the search by air. PC Whalley must have been frustrated.

Had Cregan slipped through his grasp? It was true the one-eyed fugitive had been in Failsworth. But the police investigation would later establish that the man he had chased and who had been so determined to evade capture wasn't Cregan at all but someone else.

A ne'er-do-well, no doubt, but not a murderer. Not Public Enemy No.1. Amid the inevitable confusion of a huge manhunt which was in its infancy, one thing was still painfully clear: Cregan was still at large.

In fact, he and his fellow assassins were still in Failsworth, holed up at Press 2 Impress, a laundry business on Lord Lane.

WHITE HEAT

They were busy making arrangements to escape to Yorkshire with the help of friends. They must have been feeling very pleased with themselves. Mark Short was dead. David Short was dead. The Hark family home had been visited.

And Cregan – as his murder trial would later be told – had left his 'calling card'.

Cregan, Wilkinson and Ward were then helped further by Mohammed Imran Ali – known as 'Irish Immie' – who was to transport the three assassins out of Manchester and into Yorkshire until the dust had settled.

A further friend of Cregan's, Francis Dixon, was also accused of the murder of David Short, the attempted murder of Sharon Hark and causing an explosion with a hand grenade.

Although he was not present at the time David Short was killed, Dixon – a notorious career criminal in his own right – was accused of being aware of what Cregan was up to and protecting David Short's killers before and after the event.

He was eventually acquitted.

In the meantime, Cregan, Wilkinson and Ward were picked up at Press 2 Impress by Ali, who transported them across the county border to Bradford.

Yet despite breathing a sigh of relief after pulling off the mission, Cregan had not been nearly half as clever as he liked to think.

Had his wake not been so strewn with tragedy, the clues he left behind for the police would be almost comical.

Amazingly, he and his henchmen had stopped off to buy ice lollies after the murder – leaving their saliva and, crucially, their DNA, all over the wrappers found in or near their getaway car.

In the Ford Fiesta car, Cregan's DNA was found on a Mr Freeze ice lolly wrapper in the centre console. More wrappers found dumped in the front passenger door and on the floor at the back of the car had Wilkinson and Ward's DNA.

Cregan and Wilkinson had also left their fingerprints all over the inside of the Fiesta, in which they had also left empty ammunition cases and a gun magazine.

The assassins had left more clues at Luke Road: Wilkinson's DNA was found on a grenade firing pin and also on a half-eaten sandwich found in the back of the Vauxhall Combo van. All three left their DNA on water bottles they drank from while in the van.

They also left fingerprints in the van, as well as a fired gun cartridge and nine unused 9mm rounds. Cregan had wrongly assumed the grenade would obliterate all the evidence inside the van. And they had not counted on police finding the Ford Fiesta. Although the planning was detailed, the gang's sloppiness in executing it would help to nail them in the end.

With the assassins long gone, police took a bold step.

At 6pm, Assistant Chief Constable Garry Shewan stepped out of GMP's Nexus House complex, about a mile from where David Short had been murdered, and read out a prepared script in which he named Dale Cregan as a suspect in the murder, and the murder of Short's son, Mark.

Not many journalists had gathered for the briefing, perhaps half a dozen including reporters from the Manchester Evening News and local radio stations. National newspapers had not shown much interest to that point, with the notable exception of Russell Jenkins from The Times who looked incongruous at the scene in Clayton.

He very quickly judged this wasn't the kind of story his news editor, or readers, would be interested in and turned on his heels.

The fact the nation's attention was on a summer of sport was a source of some consternation among detectives hunting for Cregan.

The London-centric national media were more interested in Usain Bolt and the Olympics than a one-eyed fugitive from Manchester.

This story, perhaps, was just a bit too 'Shameless' for those enjoying breakfast somewhere in the Home Counties.

Whatever the judgement of news editors in London, their attitudes were about to shift.

A few moments after Shewan had named Cregan, the force emailed out a picture of the wanted man.

Those news editors in London quickly re-evaluated the story.

Before, a violent spat between two crime families barely registered even if a grenade had been used.

Now it was different.

There was a startling picture to go with the story. There was a 'one-eyed fugitive' out there, a bogey man who begged to be demonised.

And they set about it with some gusto.

7.

ESCAPE TO YORKSHIRE

Like almost everyone else in the nation, Cregan was gripped by the TV news.

Bulletins about the 'one-eyed fugitive' who was on the run and wanted for murdering a father and son left him excited and he found the drama being described on the telly all rather amusing.

After blasting David Short, he and his accomplices spent almost two weeks on the run, most of it in modern one-bed apartment in Leeds city centre, with the TV on, the lights out and the curtains drawn.

Rather than being worried though, he took a perverse pride in a reward – at that time £25,000 – being offered for information leading to his arrest. Such was the fear he inspired, he wasn't concerned a grass somewhere would go to the police and reveal his location.

He was correct to think the reward was unusual. Such huge sums had been offered before but typically only for information leading to a conviction. Here, the cash was being offered for a tit-bit that would lead to merely his capture. It was 'rare', Cregan correctly noted.

Meanwhile, hundreds of police officers, some drafted from up and down the country, were heading to Manchester as part of what had become an unprecedented manhunt.

Dozens of armed police raids were taking place across Manchester, but to no avail. He wasn't there. The search concentrated on Manchester, where Cregan could rely on a network of criminal friends to protect him, but also spread its wings across the country and even abroad.

And what the police didn't know was that Cregan had been driven up the M62 to west Yorkshire by Irish Immie.

There, it seemed he and Wilkinson were being waited on by their first getaway driver-cum-slave, Jermaine Ward. Irish Immie brought them supplies, so they never had to leave the flat.

Only the sound of a passing police siren prompted them to look behind the curtains to see what was going on. They did some drugs, drank beer and watched TV, especially the news bulletins.

When a tribute to the murdered Shorts came on the news – in which the fallen father-and-son were described as 'lions' – Cregan laughed out loud. "They didn't look like lions to me," he said.

It was clear he had taken pleasure in murdering both.

Whether or not his victims had been 'lions', Cregan had not exactly acted nobly – all his four murder victims, the Shorts as well as the two PCs he would go on to slaughter, were unarmed and were taken by surprise before they could do anything to defend themselves.

Perhaps bored, the trio headed to the south coast. They spent a few days 'chillin' as Cregan put it, and drinking at Herne Bay, not far from Dover, where they no doubt considered making a dash across The Channel. It would have been particularly dangerous for Cregan and Wilkinson, whose mugshots had been splashed all across the papers as part of the police hunt.

There was another problem for Wilkinson – he had forgotten his passport. He had left it on a table at his mother's house in Beswick.

Life for the fugitive trio slowly began to unravel and on August 23, 2012, nearly two weeks after the killing of David Short, the getaway driver for that crime had tired of life on the run.

Jermaine Ward walked into Huddersfield police station shortly after midnight, and he wanted to talk. The 24-year-old first insisted that his mother and brother were safe before he said anything.

Cregan had threatened to kill them, and him, if he went to the authorities, he claimed.

Cregan had forced a grenade into his mouth.

Armed police were dispatched to his mum's house and to The Christie hospital in Manchester, where his brother was being treated for cancer.

Ward then spent the next two days giving police details of the murder of David Short, and the plush apartment in Leeds he rather ludicrously described as a 'dungeon'.

He said he'd been terrorised and forced to take part in the murder under duress and had then been held hostage.

After walking into the police station, Ward said he'd just been dumped out on the Yorkshire moors after being kicked out of a van by the laughing Cregan and Wilkinson, and he wanted to spill the beans. Cregan and Wilkinson, however, remained on the run and Ward insisted he had no idea where they were hiding. It seemed he wasn't tempted to claim the £25,000 reward.

He claimed he had been forced by Cregan at gunpoint to do his bidding. In fact, he had been a trusted and central part of the plot. And Cregan had simply tired of Ward after spending two weeks holed up with him.

Cregan would later tell a psychologist who visited him in prison he had considered killing Ward but could not come up with a valid reason to act on his impulse. After all, Ward had done everything asked of him.

The police never fell for Ward's sob story.

The tears which flowed were crocodile tears, as far as the interviewing police officers were concerned.

Ward, one of five brothers, was transported from the station at Huddersfield back to Manchester, and over the next two days of extensive police interviews, he would give a rambling, often tearful account of what had happened. Whether what he said was the whole truth, partly the truth or a concoction, his story was undoubtedly a rare insight into the way Cregan operated.

Initially, at least, there was no sign of Cregan, the murderous monster.

ESCAPE TO YORKSHIRE

Ward painted a picture of Cregan as a generous and house-proud friend. He said he'd known Cregan socially for about two years. He was a 'decent guy who was always offering me a drink'.

When Cregan had guests at his house he was 'always telling people to be quiet and to stop taking the piss'. "He didn't seem like a hard man to me or a gangster," said Ward.

The events of the two weeks before walking into the nick in Huddersfield had forced Ward to re-evaluate his friend. He claimed he was another victim of Dale Cregan's brutality, and on three or four occasions had a grenade forced into his mouth while held captive. He had been tortured mentally and physically, he said. Cregan had pressed a red-hot spoon into his shoulder.

He had spent the night before the murder of David Short at a house in Beswick, a tough estate east of Manchester.

It was Wilkinson's mother's house.

On the day of the murder, Ward claimed he thought his generous friend Cregan would be giving him a lift to Bolton Crown Court where he faced sentencing for producing amphetamines on an industrial scale.

Instead of going to court, he said Cregan offered him £50 to pick up a hire van to be used in the murder that was to come, and he was recruited to act as his first getaway driver.

Ward claimed not to know why Cregan and Wilkinson had first staked out the cemetery as they waited for David Short to show up, and nor did he ask: "I didn't have a clue what we was doing. I didn't know if we were going to rob someone. I didn't have a clue. I heard them saying 'shall we stay here or shall we go?'."

He broke down in tears on several occasions as he tried to explain to the police why he had allowed himself to take part in the David Short murder.

Moments before the slaughter, Cregan had rammed a gun to the side of his head and said 'I'll kill you. I'll shoot you right now if you try something'.

Ward told police: "At first I had a nervous laugh. I was shocked. I said 'are you joking?' and he laughed and said 'do I look like I'm fucking joking?' and he rammed the gun into the side of my head. He was talking about my brother, saying he would go and shoot him, and I knew he wasn't mucking about. My heart sank. I felt paralysed. I was caught up in the middle of everything. I thought 'do I deserve this? Does my family deserve this?'. I could see him looking around in a bag with grenades inside it. He passed a gun to Anthony. It was like nothing I have ever seen before. There were grenades and a lot of bullets. I just felt like I had to (drive). He was saying 'if you don't do it I'll shoot you right now and go to your house and kill your mam. Do I look like I'm fucking joking, nigger?' I was told not to drive fast, just to drive normally."

He described how Cregan and Wilkinson returned to the van after committing the murder, although Ward professed he had no idea about the horrific crime they had just carried out despite the spots of Short's blood on Cregan's shirt.

He claimed only to have realised murder had been committed on the TV news while the gang was holed up in Leeds.

"I heard numerous bangs and then another loud bang and then there was smoke and then it was like 'drive, drive'," he said.

Dale had blood on his face and a speck of blood on his shirt. I knew something had happened. He was shouting 'drive, drive'. I was shocked. I couldn't drive properly. He said 'I told you, just drive, drive now'. My legs were shaking. I couldn't properly move and when I eventually started to drive, he told me this way or that. They were just laughing at each other, touching each other's hands.

"I didn't have a clue. I just seen them get into the back of the van. I wasn't thinking about it. I wasn't bothered about what they had done. I was bothered about my family. It didn't enter my head. Obviously, I knew they had done something. Obviously, I had seen blood on him. I didn't ask questions.

"I was concentrating on my own life. I didn't have a clue what had happened. They had done something to someone. Obviously, they had shot someone. I don't know. As soon as they were back in the van, they were telling me to drive. I wasn't really bothered about what he had done. I was concentrating on myself."

He then drove the pair to Luke Road in nearby Droylsden where Cregan tossed a grenade at Sharon Hark's house.

Ward carried Cregan's heavy bag of munitions across Lees Park but claimed to be unclear about the contents. "I don't know. Bullets. Grenades. Guns. Anything," said Ward when he was asked what he thought was inside the bag, which was heavy and clanking noisily as he made his way across the park.

Ward ferried the two hitmen north to Press 2 Impress, where they cleaned up and got ready to get out of the city and head to Yorkshire. According to Ward, not a word was spoken on the journey to Failsworth. Silence.

It wasn't a picture police recognised.

They imagined the three assassins being rather pleased with their successful mission, even ecstatic. They had just killed David Short, one of the most feared men in Manchester.

After they had cleaned up and finished congratulating each other, the three assassins were picked up by Irish Immie, who drove them to the 'dungeon' in Leeds. Actually, it was plush apartment in the Faroe Building in the city.

It seems no-one there noticed that Britain's most wanted man was among them. There, the trio remained holed up for days. Cregan and Wilkinson, according to Ward, regularly watched news bulletins in the flat to keep up with events in Manchester.

Ward claimed that it was only when the news showed CCTV of the grenade attack at Luke Road that he recognised the two figures in the footage as Cregan and Wilkinson.

The report had said a gun was fired at the property but Cregan insisted it had jammed. "They were just laughing at it like it was a joke," he said.

Ward claimed he was their domestic slave, preparing their food and washing their dishes, in the 'dungeon'. Although police later established its precise location, Ward professed to have no idea where it was except that it was a flat on an estate somewhere.

He claimed had been driven there in the back of a car in the hours after the David Short murder. The car was reversed up to the door of the flat before he had a jumper pulled over his head and was bundled into the apartment. It was all part of his effort to make sure the trail back to Cregan and Wilkinson went cold.

Ward said he did not realise what was happening when he claimed he saw Cregan and Wilkinson cooking something on the spoon, which drew incredulity from the interviewing officers. He described how, apparently for fun, Cregan pressed a gun to his head and pulled the trigger. "It went click. I didn't know there was nothing in it," said Ward as he wept again.

Cregan kept a stack of £20 notes in the flat and would discuss plans to escape to Cork or possibly Dublin, suggested Ward.

The police who interviewed him were never persuaded by the story.

Why had he not simply driven away in the van while Cregan and Wilkinson were murdering David Short? Why did he not make a run for it when he was carrying the bag of munitions across Lees Park?

Why did he not sneak out of the flat in Leeds while his alleged captors were sleeping? Why had he failed to take advantage of the many chances, even on his own account, he had to escape?

There were more tears as he tried to explain: "It never crossed my mind to even try (to sneak out of the flat). They were always keeping their eye on me and checking. They always had a gun by their sides. They had a grenade in my mouth. It never crossed my mind to try to get away. They were always looking out around the curtains when they heard sirens. They would be uncertain and looking around doors. Most of the time one was asleep and the other was awake. Most of the time I pretended to be asleep so that I didn't feel as though I was in their way or anything. I didn't have keys. I didn't know where the keys were. I didn't know if the door was locked on the inside. I didn't go to the front door to try. I didn't want to try. I just wanted to do what they said. It was like a dungeon. It was dark. They sat with the lights out and the telly on. I just tried to keep myself to myself and tried to keep them happy.

"If I had got away, I don't know whether they would have gone to the hospital to kill my brother who's got cancer. I didn't know what to do. They could have killed my brother. If I did get away, they could have taken a gun to the hospital to kill my brother."

He could not explain why Cregan and Wilkinson, according to his story, had suddenly decided to take him out onto the moors in their van and kick him out. He told police he had walked all the way to Huddersfield Police Station. "I didn't know if they were taking me somewhere to kill me. I didn't hear them saying 'you are going here or there'. The first I knew, they were saying 'come on, you're going'."

It was only at the very end of his lengthy police interview that a world-weary Manchester detective told him exactly what he thought of his story.

Detective Constable Chris Barnes laid his cards on the table.

He said: "I think he (Cregan) trusted you. I think you were a willing accomplice in all this. I think you drove that van quite willingly, probably for payment."

Ward (sobbing) said: "That's when my life changed."

Det Con Barnes: "Getaway drivers for villains are a very big commodity. They are the most trusted people. You can give any muppet a gun. You need someone you trust, someone who you put your life in their hands, to be a getaway driver."

Ward: "I was worried about my brother. He's got cancer."

Det Con Barnes: "Dale Cregan has been a villain all his life. He doesn't get caught because people won't give evidence against him. He's not stupid. He covers his tracks, right? He's not going to use someone who's afraid and cannot drive, is he?"

Ward: "I could not drive. I could drive but I could not drive away. I couldn't get into gear most of the time."

Accused of handling one of the guns used in the murder of David Short, Ward said: "I have never held a gun. I wouldn't know what to do with a gun."

Det Con Barnes: "I think you are trying to minimise your role in all this."

Ward: "I'm not lying about anything. I have told you everything. I came to the police station when I first could. He put a gun to my head. If he put a grenade in your mouth, you would feel it."

Det Con Barnes: "People don't kill other people, get in a van, go in a Ford Fiesta and drive to Yorkshire and not talk about it. You are there next to them. It doesn't happen. It doesn't happen. I think you have had conversations. You just won't tell us."

Ward: "I have told you what I know, what I have heard. I have told you what I can. I have told you."

Det Con Barnes: "If you can tell me where they are, how I can find them, it can only do you the power of good."

Ward: "What I can tell you about him, I have told you."

Det Con Barnes: "Are you protecting anybody else?"

Ward: "I'm just worried about my family, about their safety now."

Det Con Barnes wasn't the only one to be utterly unconvinced by the performance.

The way Ward had handed himself in to police and was happily co-operating with them, was in stark contrast to Cregan and Wilkinson.

Until, finally, Wilkinson grew tired of life on the run.

He too would come in quietly.

He too would come in without causing bloodshed and carnage.

Before long, Cregan would be the only man still out on the streets.

8.

KILL OR
BE KILLED

Anthony Wilkinson hobbled away from the scene of David
Short's murder after a piece of shrapnel from Cregan's grenade
struck his foot.

It was a minor inconvenience for a man who had told his
family he was prepared to die as he carried out the killing with
his friend Cregan.

It was 'kill or be killed' as far as he was concerned.

He believed he had to kill David Short because he had
threatened to murder him and his two sons.

Even if David Short didn't get to him first, he was sure a
police marksmen would do the job.

Even after he and Cregan had obliterated their enemy's body
in a hail of bullets and grenade explosions, Wilkinson's anger
barely subsided.

"Tell that John Short there's more where that came from," he would eventually tell police while he was sitting in his cell and thinking about the possibility of a very long stretch inside. Wilkinson was probably referring to John Short, aka John Collins, a member of the extended Short family, who had been shot in the Cotton Tree and was lucky to survive, although it may have been directed at David Short's brother, also John.

For a man so full of hate Anthony Wilkinson was also very full of apologies. He was sorry.

Very, very sorry. In a letter to his former partner Lucy Latham, the mother of his two sons, Wilkinson couldn't stop apologising. Not for shooting dead David Short. He certainly wasn't sorry for that. No, what he felt bad about was how the whole drama had affected his fragmented family. So, a grovelling letter of apology to his ex and the gift of a £400 designer watch for his son were supposed to go some way towards making amends.

The letter had been written in the weeks after the murder of Short snr while Wilkinson was on the run with Cregan, holed up in Leeds.

The mugshots of both had become familiar features in newspaper and TV reports about the huge rewards on offer for information leading to the arrest of his killers. The police were paying daily visits to the families of both fugitives, keeping up the pressure on the two men in the hope they would hand themselves into the police without any trouble.

As part of the continuing police operation, officers searched Lucy Latham's house on September 2. She knew police would find the letter her former partner had sent her so she handed it over. Her mistake had been not to burn the letter as his note had suggested.

It appeared to be addressed to Wilkinson's sons as well as his ex.

In it, he wrote: "I'm sorry about everything. Don't be scared. No-one will ever hurt you or my boys. Hope you trust me on that. I can't contact you. The police are listening to every call. All I can say is I'm sorry. Love you and my kids. I love you very much. Don't tell anyone you have been in contact or I will be in shit. Burn this letter and don't speak in houses. I think they will shoot us if they get us, the police. So if they do, look after my boys. Money will be getting dropped off for you. Sorry."

Later in the letter, appearing to address his sons, he wrote: "It's dad. I'm sorry about all this. (It) don't mean I don't love you. You mean the world to me... I'm sorry. I can't speak to you yet but will ring you when I can.. I still love you. Things might come off for us yet." He ended the letter by asking his former partner to give Ryan one of his watches, pointing out it cost him £400, and insisting 'don't let Ryan go down Clayton', in case he bumped into any of the Shorts.

In the end, Wilkinson was nailed – in part – by his own stepmother. He had confided in her that he would ensure the grieving David Short would soon join his murdered son Mark in his plot at Droylsden Cemetery.

She thought it had been an idle, unfounded boast until she heard Short snr had been slaughtered. She knew her stepson had been involved and called 999.

Marion Wilkinson was terrified even as she dialled the authorities.

Police call-handler Lidia Sarno was on duty in the Old Trafford control room of Greater Manchester Police on the morning of August 10.

She and her colleagues had taken a rash of calls reporting a shooting and the sound of explosions around David Short's home in Clayton, some six miles across the city.

One of the calls taken that day was from Marion at 12.48pm. The caller said she knew who was responsible for the shooting.

She did not name him but she revealed the shooter she was talking about was her late husband's son.

In fact, the shooter had told Marion he had originally planned the murder for the 8th or 9th of August.

It appears Wilkinson had considered the possibility he might die during the attack. The shooter, Marion told the call-handler, had said his goodbyes, both to his children and to his late father in the cemetery.

She at first thought they were idle threats and even when her stepson promised his yet-to-be committed crime would be 'on the news', she didn't believe him.

Before the 999 call Marion was making had even finished, an officer who was already at the scene of the second explosion, at Sharon Hark's house in Droylsden, was forwarded her mobile and location, and was sent to find her.

Detective Sergeant David Donlan picked Marion up in an unmarked police car.

She was nervous, very nervous.

She knew what she was doing would be regarded as the highest treachery by Anthony Wilkinson and others, and he would have no hesitation in killing her or her children. No words were exchanged in the car. The officer was simply told to drive. The detective drove, as requested, into Droylsden Cemetery. The venue for the chat that would follow was certainly quiet, and far enough away from the bullet-strewn crime scenes nearby for the pair to know they would not be disturbed. Or, worse, caught.

And, whether it was meant that way or not, the cemetery was also a poignant choice.

This was where Marion's late husband was buried. She visited often. And over the last three months this was where she would regularly bump into David Short, who visited his son Mark's grave there as well.

After the car had parked up just inside the cemetery gates, the woman in the passenger seat identified herself as 'Marion Wilson.' It was a feeble lie borne out of fear. It would very soon become clear exactly who she was.

She wanted to speak to the police. She didn't believe him at the time, but two weeks earlier, Wilkinson had told her he was going to murder David Short. In fact, he had told her David would be joining Mark in his grave 'very soon'.

Anthony had asked her how often David Short had visited his son's grave and she had told him: every morning. Anthony Wilkinson claimed he and his family had received death threats from David Short and it was a case of 'kill or be killed'.

Wilkinson had told her about escaping to Tenerife and had

access to a passport. She had heard rumours his friend Cregan had machine guns and hand grenades, and had even heard that Cregan had been bragging in a local pub that he was going to 'get the Shorts'.

The chat in the car came to an abrupt end soon after Marion noticed the officer was making notes. She believed she was talking to the detective confidentially. She became hysterical. If there were notes, these could be used in a prosecution and her stepson would know she had been speaking to the police. Her life would be in danger.

Det Sgt Donlan recalled: "After she had given me most of the information, she realised I was taking notes. I don't think she could see at first as I had my day book on my knee under the steering wheel, and when she saw I was taking notes, she panicked and became hysterical and wanted to get out of the vehicle."

Marion never wavered from her insistence that there was no way she would give evidence in court. When she was pressed about giving evidence, she told police: "I would rather top myself than go to court."

She said she had tried to kill herself twice since the murder of David Short and that she had now been branded a 'grassing cunt' after news of her dialogue with the investigation had leaked out. She was clear: if she was summonsed to appear in the trial, she would 'take a load of sleeping pills and the police could deal with that'.

She wasn't the only person who had been told that murder was on Wilkinson's mind.

His former love, Lucy Latham, had spoken to Marion within hours of David Short's murder and said: "So he did it then." The 'it' she had referred to had been made crystal clear to her by Wilkinson when he visited her out-of-the-blue the day before the murder.

Unexpected, he appeared in her back garden in the afternoon. Again, it was obvious he was prepared for the possibility he may not survive the attack. "Make sure the kids will always remember me. You will see it on the news tomorrow," Wilkinson told her in the back garden, before speaking to his two sons by her. He was edgy, and for good reason. He was about to take part in one of the most horrific gangland murders Manchester had ever seen.

And, if he was to be believed, his own life and even the lives of his two sons were under threat from a grieving father seeking revenge for the murder of his own son.

In the evening, long after the visit, Wilkinson rang his ex and continued in the same vein expressing love for his sons: "Don't ever think I'm never thinking about the kids in all this. What's got to be done, has to be done. I've got tears in my eyes. I will always love them."

Wilkinson was true to his word as he callously gunned down David Short along with Cregan.

As soon as the carnage had ended, their vanishing act began.

And GMP threw everything they had at the case to try and bring about a peaceful and safe conclusion for all concerned.

9.

THE
HUNT

While a team of 60 detectives from the Major Incident Team of Greater Manchester Police were working on the investigation into the deaths of Mark and David Short, at the same time hundreds of other police officers were involved in the round-the-clock search for Cregan and Wilkinson.

In fact, the days and weeks leading up to Cregan murdering PCs Hughes and Bone were filled with exhaustive and exhausting police efforts to bring them in safely.

It wasn't unusual for officers right at the heart of the operation to be putting in 15-hour days, especially at the beginning.

GMP drew on all its own resources, and called in others.

Help came in from forces up and down the land and other law enforcement agencies. Army bomb disposal experts and forensic psychologists were in the pool of helpers doing their bit to bring the hunt to an end.

As he sat in the bolthole apartment in Leeds, Cregan toyed with the idea of making a new life for himself overseas but, in the end, police believe that he may never have left the country during the manhunt.

It would have been dangerous because almost everyone in the country – certainly Border Agency staff – were looking out for the one-eyed fugitive.

While he was on the run, he spoke about heading to Cork or Dublin. He had lived for a brief period in Tenerife in his earlier years, so that was an option, too.

In the end, he remained in the UK, and found himself drawn back to Manchester, following his initial spell in Yorkshire.

Reports even suggested a bearded Cregan was brazen enough, and confident enough, to go drinking in boozers around Tameside.

This painted a picture of a man who knew he was such a terrifying figure no-one would dare to grass him up to the police. Whether this was true or not, Manchester was certainly a magnet for Cregan.

Manchester was home, where his mates – the friends who would protect him – his mother, girlfriend and child still lived.

While he kept his head down, east Manchester was a scary place to be.

Armed police were on patrol around the clock, particularly in Drolylsden and Clayton.

Armed Response Vehicles were never more than a few minutes away from any incident if required.

As the manhunt progressed, detectives privately expressed

the fear Cregan would try to go out in a blaze of glory, either in a shootout with the police or perhaps by killing innocent members of the public.

They were worried he might even bomb a police station with his grenades.

Their instincts were right.

The talk which dominated the neighbourhoods of Clayton and Droylsden was of revenge. For many, it was a matter of when, and not if, the surviving members of the Short family, or someone close to them, went out and got their own back.

Cregan's mother, Anita, was among the 100-plus people who were handed 'threat to life' notices by the police. His girlfriend Georgia Merriman was also given one. Once called 'Osman warnings', these official documents were signed and witnessed by police officers, and countersigned by the recipient.

Whoever got one was warned they were at 'serious risk' of harm from their enemies and they should consider leaving the area. If they remained, they were urged to beef up their home security and stay with friends when they headed out. And they were warned that, while GMP would do what it could to protect them, they could offer no assurances. These startling documents were dished out like confetti in the summer of 2012.

Right at the start of the manhunt, senior officers spoke of 'significant advances' in the investigation but, in truth, they were no closer to finding the man at the heart of it all.

At the same time, a reward of £25,000 was put up to help bring the matter to a close. Unusually, the reward was offered for information leading to their arrest rather than their conviction. Police just wanted dangerous men off the streets and out of harm's way. They would worry about what evidence they had to convict them once they were locked up.

As with almost all 'gangland' crimes – and these two murders fell squarely into that category – police found that reliable information was hard to find. When they did find it, getting someone to sign a witness statement and then persuading them to give evidence in court were frequently insurmountable obstacles. People were just too scared.

There were plenty of civic-minded people who were willing to help, but typically they just didn't possess the kind of information that would be crucial to the investigation or the manhunt. There was also another category of potential witnesses – criminals and their associates – who did their utmost to thwart a police investigation in order to help their mates.

They might have been frightened too, but primarily they just wanted to ensure Cregan and Wilkinson remained one step ahead of the law. Both these men, police believed, were allowed to remain at large for so long because of a 'criminal conspiracy' protecting them.

All the time they were on the run, they had to sleep somewhere. They needed food. They needed help. They couldn't do it on their own.

A network of criminal friends were protecting the two fugitives. Assistant Chief Constable Steve Heywood – the man GMP had put in charge of the manhunt – expressed frustration at the wall of silence his operation was coming up against: "Over the past week, we have been carrying out a thorough and significant police investigation into the circumstances surrounding the murder of David Short. While we have been pursuing a number of lines of inquiry, we believe that there are people out there who have information that can help us trace Cregan and Wilkinson, but are not helping us, for whatever reason. I want to reassure these people that they can call Crimestoppers, anonymously, and I hope that the offer of a reward gives them an added incentive.

"A reward of this nature is rare for two reasons: firstly, it is available only to those who call Crimestoppers, and it is a major development for a reward to be offered in relation to an arrest only." He hoped, vainly as it turned out, someone would call the Crimestoppers hotline, which is run by an independent charity and promises anonymity, with that all-important nugget. Although plenty of calls came into Crimestoppers' Surrey bureau, most weren't significant and the trail remained cold.

Police carried out in excess of 60 armed raids on properties all over Greater Manchester to try to find the fugitives. Typical of those raids was a dramatic swoop on a couple of houses in Lancaster Road in Droylsden, not far from the home of Anita Cregan, on the evening of August 20.

A nearby street, Sunnyside Avenue, was cordoned off as part of the search. Residents had reported hearing a series of loud bangs. Had there been gunshots? Was Dale Cregan or Anthony Wilkinson in their midst?

Some of the residents feared as much.

Whatever these noises were, it turned out they had nothing to do with the wanted men.

Police would later say they had uncovered no evidence of gunfire at the scene. Neither Cregan nor Wilkinson were at either address the police had stormed that night. It wasn't the first time and it wouldn't be the last that cops went charging through a door in a fruitless search. Each raid heightened the already considerable tension.

That particular night was hot and sticky. Dozens of people spilled out onto the streets and tempers frayed. There had been reports that a vigilante group from Clayton, riding quad bikes, had been driving around Droylsden in their own hunt for the men. The atmosphere was extremely edgy, and arguments broke out among neighbours debating the rights and wrongs of the feud between the Atkinsons and the Shorts. The tension increased further when members of Cregan's family appeared at the scene. Anita Cregan was among them and in the mood for a row.

She accused a Manchester Evening News reporter of stirring up trouble with its regular updates on the police search for her son. "You're going to get people killed," she warned the reporter, who avoided the temptation to suggest that only one person had been doing any killing and that was her own son.

Not content with just having a go at a reporter, she turned her ire on the bystanders who had gathered beside police tape which blocked off Sunnyside Avenue.

By now Anita Cregan, and other members of the family, were getting used to daily visits from the police.

The police approach was 'softly, softly' but the message was clear – we want your son. Cregan's younger sister Stacey drove by the scene several times. She chatted to friends but otherwise tried to keep a low profile. Police remained at the scene for several hours, as did the bystanders. In the end, they melted back into their homes when it was obvious neither Cregan nor Wilkinson had been found.

Residents spoke to the MEN reporter, although they remained fearful and insisted on anonymity. One said: "It's really worrying when you have got kids playing out in the street. You worry that someone innocent is going to get hurt. People just want an end to it." He was right to worry. Two innocent bobbies would be murdered by Cregan a few weeks later. Another resident said: "I've lived here nearly 20 years and this is as bad as I've ever known it."

A few days later, police upped the ante. ACC Heywood went public again: "We have an unprecedented amount of officers dedicated to this case, ranging from detectives to firearms officers to CCTV officers. The operation will continue to work at this level of intensity for the foreseeable future, until we have located the two men we want to speak to in connection with these attacks. Armed officers are continuing to patrol in the Clayton and Droylsden areas, and while I appreciate people might find their appearance quite daunting, I hope they can also feel reassured by their presence."

By now GMP had hundreds of police officers working on the various strands of the investigation, and holes were beginning to appear elsewhere as officers were removed from their usual roles to help with more pressing matters. Forces from around the country sent in reinforcements to plug the gaps.

More raids were carried out in Droylsden and also Failsworth, north of Manchester, without success.

One breakthrough had occurred when Ward handed himself in and two days of interviews with him provided detectives with their first significant insight into what Cregan had been up to.

But the manhunt needed another push. In the last week of August, the reward of £25,000 was doubled to £50,000. The terms remained the same. The message to anyone who could locate them was: just tell us where they are and if we arrest them, you get the money. Only twice before had GMP offered such a large sum of money, and then only for information leading to convictions.

It was offered following two murders; for the 2006 killing of 15-year-old schoolboy Jessie James, who was gunned down in a Moss Side park; and for the Boxing Day 2011 murder of Indian student Anuj Bidve in Salford. The cash was never claimed for the still unsolved murder of Jessie James. A portion was claimed for the Anuj Bidve murder after Kieran 'Psycho' Stapleton was convicted of the killing.

ACC Garry Shewan was the officer who was put forward to make GMP's pitch: "This amount of money will allow the recipient not only to change their own lives forever, but to provide long-term financial security for their whole family.

"It is highly unusual to offer such a large sum, but we understand people are worried about their safety when providing information to the police. That is why the information can be given anonymously through Crimestoppers. We are now entering the third week of this operation and we understand that people will be impatient for results."

If the sum on offer had at least one other zero on the end of it, Shewan's pitch may have been more persuasive.

A reward of £50,000 wasn't exactly the life-changing Lottery win it was portrayed.

It wasn't really enough compensation for a life-time of looking over your shoulder.

The officers who were out looking for the two fugitives were left in no doubt it just wasn't enough money, and that perhaps no amount of money would be enough. "We'd be dead before we had the chance to spend it," was a regular refrain they heard out on the streets. Senior police were prepared to pay more.

Much more.

Although the force was in the middle of a savage cost-cutting drive, shedding some 2,700 posts as it sought to save £134m as part of the Government's drive to reduce the national debt, senior officers soon had their calculators out. The hunt for Cregan and Wilkinson was costing the force an estimated £150,000 a day.

It didn't take a mathematical genius to work out that it could be worthwhile offering a far larger sum.

As far as the taxpayer was concerned, the real cost of the operation was something far more tangible than a number with six zeros behind it. It was the victims of other crimes who would suffer, although they were unlikely to appreciate the reason why. It was the burglary investigation that was delayed or just didn't happen because officers were seconded to the ever-increasing operation to find Cregan and Wilkinson.

In those circumstances, senior officers seriously thought about a 'name your price' reward, although it never came to that.

To go along with the juicy carrot that was being dangled so publicly, police were still wielding a sizeable stick behind the scenes.

Armed police were continuing to bash down doors all across Greater Manchester. The day after the reward was doubled, police swooped on Press 2 Impress. Officers had to use an angle-grinder to get into the property, but once again Cregan had eluded them.

The main man was still at large, but a few days later, Wilkinson was finally in police custody.

On September 2, 2012, the same day as he penned his letter to Lucy Latham, he was arrested by armed police in a kids' park in Openshaw.

Officially, they had swooped after a tip-off.

In fact, Wilkinson had let it be known he was in the park. In effect, he had handed himself in.

Just like Ward two weeks earlier, Wilkinson had had enough of being on the run, of constantly looking over his shoulder.

Some of his friends had alerted armed police on patrol in the area that he was nearby in the park and wanted to be arrested.

When police eventually found him, he was asked if he had anything on him, namely weapons. His sarcastic reply was: "Only two grenades."

He wasn't armed. He knew he wouldn't be coming out of prison for some time and so, also like Cregan, he made the most of his last few hours and days of freedom with a huge drinking session.

THE HUNT

One of his chief concerns was his mother's welfare, possibly because he knew one of his guns had been found at her house.

Police had searched his mother Joan's house, where he stayed regularly, and found a 9mm Browning self-loading pistol with the safety catch off and loaded with three live rounds in the magazine.

It had been left casually on a chair in the kitchen. His passport was on a sideboard. Perhaps he had forgotten it in his haste to murder David Short. The search also uncovered a further four rounds in a nearby adidas bag. Wilkinson's DNA was found all over the weapon.

A deadly weapon, no doubt, but it had not been used in the murder of David Short. Cregan's 9mm Glock, the same one he used to kill two police officers, and an unidentified .45 calibre weapon had been used instead.

While he was at the police station, Wilkinson was thinking about what defence he might mount once his case got to court.

Before he was charged, Wilkinson asked an officer 'what's diminished responsibility?'.

Unimpressed, officers told him he wasn't mad. He replied 'I fucking am'. He complained to the officer that he had been wearing the same clothes for two weeks since he 'did the job', although he later tried to take back the comment.

On another occasion he said he had 'been on a wing' with David Short in prison, and complained about police snooping around other inmates for information.

While he was at the station, a doctor had to be called to remove something from his feet. It looked as if he had been hit by shrapnel from the grenade detonations a few weeks earlier although the injuries were only superficial.

After so many weeks on the run and three days on the beer, his language was loose and incriminating. Officers made notes about his comments and they were used as part of the later prosecution.

In hours and hours of subsequent, formal police interviews, Wilkinson was far less forthcoming than he had been in and around the cells at the station. He made no comment to the officers except to confirm the Browning 9mm gun found in his mother's house in Beswick was his.

Like Cregan, the only time he made any meaningful comment was when his manhood was challenged. Asked if he was scared of Cregan, he replied: "I'm scared of no-one."

Two down, one to go.

Cregan, the man police wanted above all others, was still the focus of a huge manhunt.

And, during their regular visits to his mother and wider family, it was suggested to police that perhaps Cregan couldn't envisage a bloodless way out of his predicament, that perhaps he thought he might be shot the moment he tried to hand himself in.

Whether Cregan himself had informed these suggestions was difficult to know for certain.

His character and mental state, however, were most definitely of interest to detectives, and they recruited the help of a forensic criminal psychologist, of the kind made famous by the 1990s ITV series Cracker. The fictional psychologist, Fitz, played by Robbie Coltrane, helped fictional detectives solve major crimes. In the real world, such expert help was only of limited value.

On its own, it would not find Cregan. But it certainly did help to set the tone of the very many public pronouncements by police.

Officers were at pains to be conciliatory, non-belligerent and even empowering, although privately they no doubt fantasized about ringing Cregan's neck. And by now police were willing to put themselves up for interview and answer questions rather than simply punt out statements through their press office.

In one such interview with the Manchester Evening News, ACC Heywood epitomised this benign public approach: "We safely arrested Anthony Wilkinson in a park in Openshaw. There was no drama, no harm to members of the public. What will now continue is daily visits to Dale Cregan's family, his friends and associates and they will continue until there is a safe resolution. Mr Cregan is aware that he's in control of the situation and he's got some options and now he needs to choose. Does he contact his solicitor and come in? Or does he contact his family and come in? Or does he contact us directly and come in safely to a police station? The common theme here is for him to come in. There's a lot of speculation among his friends and family that they are afraid that there's no safe way out of this. But what I'm saying is that there is a safe way. He can contact his friends or allies or contact us directly. My aim is to safely resolve this situation. We've done it with Anthony Wilkinson. There was no drama. He has been locked up. I want to do the same with Dale Cregan. He's wanted in connection with murder. We have to question him and then it's up to the Crown Prosecution Service what happens next." The tactic was to play up his importance, to put the ball in his court, to massage his ego.

But Cregan had other ideas.

The days passed and still there was no sign of Britain's most wanted man. Police had pretty much exhausted all the tools to hand when it came to exploiting the mainstream media, and so they turned to more inventive ways to promote the £50,000 reward on offer.

Perhaps there were others who had valuable information who simply didn't read newspapers or watch the TV news. Many of the Shorts and Atkinsons appeared to be Manchester City fans so GMP got the club to flash up a picture of the one-eyed Cregan at half-time accompanied by the sum on offer at its home games.

As the days went by, similar messages were shown at other football matches up and down the country. Trucks, mounted with huge digital billboards, toured Manchester's clubs and pubs at night. It seemed it didn't matter what tactic was adopted. There was still no breakthrough.

Yet another appeal went out on September 7, but this time the rhetoric was a little firmer and would have left Cregan in no doubt that there would be no let-up in the pressure being put on his own family while he remained at large.

ACC Shewan said: "This the fourth week since the shooting and grenade attacks in which David Short was tragically killed. Since that day, we have not relented in our high-profile policing operation. My officers have been paying regular visits to all of Dale Cregan's family members, friends and associates and the message I want to send out loud and clear is we will continue to make these visits until Dale is found.

"Dale has now been in hiding for almost a month, during which time his photo has been splashed all over the media, digital screens and advertising vans around Greater Manchester and beyond. However, I want to stress to Dale that all we want, and I'm sure all he wants too, is to find a safe way to resolve this situation. We don't want a stand-off or any drama, but just to end this peacefully. Dale can take control of this matter by speaking to a family member, friend or to his solicitor, and arrange to come into a police station or speak to the police. Dale's family are desperate to see him safe and so I would urge him to contact someone he trusts today, and work with us to end this safely."

It seemed police were now on first name terms with 'Dale'.

But the informality couldn't mask the explicit threat to continue with the daily visits to his mother, Anita, and others; visits that Cregan clearly resented, as he proved when he walked into Hyde Police Station 10 days later, having murdered two police officers.

But what were police supposed to do? Leave his mother in peace?

Or put some pressure on her to get him to hand himself in?

Cregan's family certainly pointed the finger of blame at the police. In the aftermath of the murders that followed, there would be some soul-searching at GMP about the tactics they had adopted. After all, two of their colleagues had been murdered and the murderer had blamed the police for forcing him into a corner.

There was an investigation by the Health and Safety Executive. GMP is nothing if not adept when it comes to self-flagellation, so a period of introspection followed.

For all its well-documented flaws, it didn't take long for senior officers at GMP to come to the very firm conclusion that they had acted properly.

The visits were regular and the message was clear – let's get 'Dale' into custody. According to the police, the tone of those visits had never been threatening and, if anything, the officers were obliging and helpful, asking 'Anita' what they could do for her. Why would they want to overtly antagonise one of the few people who could help bring him in?

Nonetheless, she kept a diary of the daily police visits.

Later, the detectives at the centre of the manhunt simply didn't recognise the picture painted by either Cregan or his mother.

One senior officer said: "The dealings with her certainly weren't oppressive. They were trying to encourage her to engage with us, to let us know whether she had been on contact with Dale and about saying to her 'we need to get Dale in but we want to do it in a safe manner'. I just don't recognise his view that it was in any way oppressive. She was certainly seen regularly as were many people in order to try to find him. It was constructive. She was offered any assistance she needed in terms of trying to get in touch with him, trying to get him in in a safe manner. He represented us as some kind of threat which is simply not the case."

The officer gave an insight into the pressures the police were feeling as the manhunt continued: "I've been here 20 years and it was the most intense period of policing I have been through. We just got every resource we could into the manhunt. We tried every single thing we could, every tactic or technique we could think of to find out where they were. And that was constantly the case throughout the period of the manhunt. For the first week we were working regular 15, 16 or 17-hour days. There was a murder investigation and, on top of that, a manhunt.

"You do feel pressure, but it's self-imposed. You want to do the best job you can. Michelle Kelly had lost her son and her husband or partner. It's the same on any murder. You want to do the best you can for the victims and their families. We always say we are their representatives. We are the only ones who can get justice for them and we want to do our best. But with it there's the added pressure of trying to find Cregan with the risk he clearly posed to particular individuals and the public in general."

Eventually, the hours, toil, cost and efforts of GMP and the plethora of other agencies used in trying to find Cregan came to nothing.

Like Ward and Wilkinson, he had finally had enough of life on the run. Of the police asking too many questions.

He knew it was time to end it.

But Cregan believed that he and he alone would write that ending.

So he took a family hostage in Mottram, he pretended to be Adam Gartree and he set the trap.

The fates of PCs Nicola Hughes and Fiona Bone had been decided.

AMBUSH

10.

THE
MURDERS

Before the police officers got the chance to knock on the front door of the three-bedroomed maisonette in Abbey Gardens, Cregan opened the front door and unleashed a hail of bullets.

They had been ambushed.

To say he simply shot the two officers, however, doesn't give the merest hint of the level of violence he used.

Any one of the 32 shots he fired from his Glock – with its extended magazine – could have killed either officer.

Parts of the attack were so gratuitous as to defy belief.

It was only after the murders that forensic analysis of the crime scene would shine a light on just how violent the killings were.

As he opened the front door to confront the approaching officers, he blasted them both in the chest.

The only reason they didn't perish there and then was because they were wearing body armour.

Both officers made a run for it.

PC Bone tried to dart to the side across the front garden while her colleague turned back up the path.

They didn't get far.

More shots were fired at them. A shot to PC Hughes' back severed her spinal cord and she collapsed, paralysed.

She was shot three more times either as she fell or while laying face down on the path.

Cregan then turned to PC Bone, who he had trapped in front of the lounge window through which he had seen the officers arriving. He fired another 24 shots at her. Some missed.

The brave officer fought back.

Somehow, she managed to draw her Taser stun gun, which was no match for Cregan's Glock.

The stun gun can only fire cables charged with electricity to stop a target in his or her tracks. She pulled the trigger but hit the pavement rather than Cregan. In all she suffered eight gunshot wounds. Most of the bullets Cregan had fired at her were stopped by her body armour or hit the wall of the house. But one of those bullets penetrated a gap in the side of the body armour under her arm and caused fatal injuries to her heart.

PC Bone defied every natural instinct to save herself.

In fact, she died trying to save her colleague.

Even though by now she had been blasted repeatedly in her body armour, she stayed and tried to help her fallen fellow officer. The fatal injury to her side suggested she had adopted the classic side-on stance she had been taught in training, where the palm of one hand is raised and the target is ordered to stop.

Detectives who investigated the murder would later marvel at the bravery shown by both officers, but particularly PC Bone.

Despite the fact both police officers were dying in front of him, Cregan's assault had not yet run its course.

He turned again to PC Hughes who was by now face-down, motionless and bleeding heavily on the pavement.

Her bright purple fingernails stood out amid the mayhem.

Cregan lowered the gun to the back of her head and fired three more shots. In total she had been shot eight times.

Still the carnage wasn't over.

Just before he fled, Cregan threw a grenade and ran. It detonated in the garden where the officers lay dying. It landed closest to PC Hughes, further harming her already terribly injured body.

The cul-de-sac echoed to the sound of gunfire and an exploding grenade, terrifying everyone who lived there. Neighbours who saw Cregan told how he seemed oblivious to everything else around him. He didn't care that he might be seen.

He was interested only in the kill.

Kayleigh Bowers was on a laptop when she heard a noise. When she went to investigate the 'fireworks' she heard, she saw Cregan pointing his Glock towards the ground and repeatedly firing at his target. The witness would not realise until later that Cregan was shooting a police officer who was already on the ground and dying. The officer the witness could not see was

PC Nicola Hughes. Cregan was firing repeatedly into the back of her head.

Kayleigh was matter-of-fact when she told police what she saw: "At first I thought it was just fireworks. Then there were another couple of bangs that didn't sound like fireworks. I got up from my chair and from the front window I could see a man standing in the front garden. He had small black gun in his right hand. The gun was pointing downwards and he was shooting as he was standing in front of a brick wall of the porch. I saw him shoot the gun about six times towards the ground. He just kind of seemed to know what he was doing. He didn't seem to look around to see if anybody was there and just concentrated on what he was doing. At the time I didn't realise what he was actually doing. At first I just thought it was somebody just messing about with a gun. I could not see anybody on the ground. I had no idea what the man was shooting at.

"I saw the man take something out of his right-hand-side jacket pocket. My first reaction was that it was a grenade. It was only the size of his hand. I saw him pull something out of it, which to me was the pin. He threw it in an overarm action towards a neighbour's house and it landed next to the fence. Then I saw the man turn and run towards the top of the street. I saw some smoke and heard a very loud bang."

Her mother, Joanne Bowers, was trying to ignore the noise as she attempted to get to sleep after a night shift as a care assistant: "I was just drifting off to sleep when I heard banging. It sounded like fireworks. Then I heard a similar noise again. I thought 'I don't believe this' as I felt irritated. Then I heard it a third time. I thought 'I'm not having this' and then I heard it a fourth time. Then there were several loud bangs in quick succession. I looked out of the window and heard another bang. I could see the man standing on the paved area near a police van on a cobbled parking area.

"The man was standing side-on to me, stooping and looking down at the floor. He stepped forwards slightly looking down at the floor intensely. His right arm was straight out in front of him at 45 degrees from his body. I saw what I thought was a gun. I saw the man hold the position for about 20 seconds and then I heard another loud bang. I can't be certain exactly what he was doing. I was shocked. I remember his face. He was unaware of anything else around him. I heard a second loud bang and the man turned and jumped over a wall. I could see he was holding something in his hands. He didn't look up. He was concentrating on whatever it was he was doing. I wondered whether he was interfering with a car. Then I saw him step forwards a couple of paces and saw him throw something towards the garden and then he crouched down by the driver's side of the car. It was as if he was aiming towards the garden. The object landed about a foot from the gate. It exploded as it hit the floor. I saw a flash of light followed by a bang. It was deafening; louder than anything I had ever heard."

Cregan dropped his Glock near the fallen officers, having emptied the magazine.

He ran back into the house where he had spent the night, grabbed car keys and fled in a BMW parked outside.

Cregan's hostage, Alan Whitwell, watched in horror as

Cregan burst out of the front door firing his Glock before joining his partner and her daughter upstairs. "I just couldn't believe it... I was hugging Lisa, looking out of the window and I could see him getting into her car and driving away. It was then I called the police," he said. Then, he heard the explosion.

Cregan hurtled out of the cul-de-sac in the BMW belonging to Whitwell's girlfriend, driving at speeds up to 100mph along the M67 to Hyde Police Station three miles away.

"I honestly believe one of us would have been killed if we had not done what we were told," Whitwell later told police. "I knew Cregan was wanted by the police for two murders. People had been shot and grenades were thrown. Any one of us could have been killed. I was going to do anything he told me to do so that he could get away as quickly as possible."

Two bodies lay motionless and bleeding – one face down on the footpath leading from the front door, and the other in a heap close to the front window.

Soon after, a breathless detective knocked on the door of a conference room at Ashton-under-Lyne Police Station a few miles away in Mottram.

He had news. Unconfirmed reports suggested Dale Cregan had just handed himself at Hyde police station a mile due south.

For an all too brief period, the officers in that room – including the most senior police officer on the division, Chief Superintendent Nick Adderley – clutched to the notion that the nation's biggest ever manhunt had just come to an end without bloodshed.

Those thoughts evaporated over the next few terrible minutes.

THE MURDERS

The officers hurried across the hall into Chief Supt Adderley's private office where he switched on the police radio handset on his desk. They were powerless to do anything as each detail of an emerging picture came into focus.

Cregan's terrible final crimes would very soon become apparent.

Slowly, detail after painful detail revealed itself. Yes, it seemed they had Cregan. But there had been reports of gunfire at Abbey Gardens in Mottram. Two police officers had been sent there to a report of an attempted burglary. Those two officers were not responding to repeated calls to their radios.

As they lay dead or dying in Abbey Gardens, the radios of PCs Bone and Hughes crackled repeatedly with a forlorn request from the police control room. With each message to the officers' call-sign, the call-handler must have feared the worst. Just silence.

"Golf Mike 41. Please respond. Golf Mike 41. Please respond."

Using GPS built into the radios, it was clear from a map on the computer screen back at the police control room that their radios were at the same spot in Abbey Gardens and weren't moving.

A back-up patrol was scrambled. Two colleagues – workmates and friends – headed out to Mottram.

Before they arrived, they had learned from their own police radio that Cregan had handed himself in, that there had been reports of gunfire in Abbey Gardens and that PCs Bone and Hughes were not answering their radios.

When the officers got there, they found a neighbour using a

towel to desperately try and stem the bleeding from a wound suffered by PC Hughes.

One of the arriving officers, a WPC, took over the vain attempts to stop the bleeding from her stomach; a gaping exit wound caused by the bullet which had gone through her back. The second officer, a male PC, tended to PC Bone and removed her stab vest.

But it was useless. It was clear she was dead.

Paramedics arrived and took over the care of PC Hughes both at the scene and in the ambulance on the way to hospital. It was a minor miracle she appeared to have been able to cling onto life for so long and although she fought hard, death was formally pronounced at the hospital.

The two colleagues, and others, who arrived at the scene to find their two friends dead or dying would struggle to come to terms with what they witnessed. For one, who was determined to get back to work months later, the simple act of putting on their uniform would prove too much, and their earnest desire to return to the beat was thwarted.

No matter what rank, high or low, officers would be tormented by feelings of guilt to go along with the awful grief and barely concealed anger.

The truth was it could very easily had been any of the 16 other 'response' officers on duty in Tameside that day or, for that matter, other colleagues who made it their business to get their hands dirty out on the beat.

It just happened to be PCs Nicola Hughes and Fiona Bone.

As he sped to the station – and as he had done after each of

Dale Cregan's mugshot, taken after he handed himself in

The Cotton Tree pub, where the summer of bloodshed began

CCTV caught Cregan firing his weapon at Sharon Hark's home

Gregan's stash of 'pineapples', discovered shortly after he was jailed for life

Police descended on Abbey Gardens following Cregan's shooting spree

Hyde Police Station. Cregan raced here at speeds exceeding 100mph after murdering PCs Hughes and Bone

PC Fiona Bone

PC Nicola Hughes

Officers from across GMP stopped
to pay tribute to their fellow officers

Right: The tears flowed as PC Fiona
Bona was laid to rest

Manchester's streets came to a standstill in October
as the city mourned the two murdered police officers

Escorting Cregan and his co-defendants to Preston Crown Court every day proved to be an enormous task

Joan and Paul Bone, the parents of PC Fiona Bone

Armed officers at Preston Crown Court were ready for any eventuality

Natalie and Bryn Hughes, the stepmother and father of PC Nicola Hughes

GMP Chief Constable Sir Peter Fahy

Left: Luke Livesey and Damien Gorman

Below: Mohammed Imran Ali, Jermaine Ward and Anthony Wilkinson

his four murders – Dale Cregan called his girlfriend Georgia Merriman.

There was a swagger in his step as he walked into Hyde Police Station. He appeared calm and casual when he walked into the front desk, telling the counter clerk: "I'm wanted by the police and I've just done two coppers."

The first police officer on the scene was PC John Snelson, who initially had merely wanted to speak to Cregan about the reckless manner in which his BMW had sped into the station's car park. The officer's heart must have skipped a beat when he recognised it was the man he and his colleagues had been hunting for the previous 42 days. Cregan, still talking to his girlfriend on the mobile held between his shoulder and ear, stretched out his arms so he could be handcuffed. The officer tried in vain to radio his colleagues but the airways were by now jammed with traffic about the murder of his two colleagues up the road.

Asked whether he was armed, Cregan made a startling admission in his broad Manchester accent: "I dropped the gun at the scene and I've murdered two police officers. You were hounding my family so I took it out on yous."

When he was arrested, Cregan admitted he had let a grenade off and expressed regret for the first and last time relating to his murder spree over the previous five months. He had not counted on killing two women. "Sorry about those two that have been killed. I wish it was men," he said.

The bomb squad was turned out and made sure the BMW in which Cregan had arrived had not been booby trapped. It hadn't. During hours and hours of police interviews, Cregan responded 'no comment' or without saying anything at all. He couldn't 'be arsed to keep saying no comment'. It was only when an interviewing officer suggested he had been a coward for not waiting for armed police to arrive at Abbey Gardens that he was stung into his first meaningful reply. "Cos yous couldn't fucking find me could yous so," he said.

Within an hour of the shooting, news was emerging of the killings and that Dale Cregan was at last in police custody.

The hunt was over – but at a terrible cost.

As Cregan was sitting in his police cell in Newton Heath, the media were gathering for a press conference at the HQ of Greater Manchester Police. Grim-faced, the Chief Constable, Sir Peter Fahy, confirmed the deaths of two of his officers, and months – if not years – of grieving would begin.

It was one of his force's 'darkest days', he said. The police family had been 'shattered by this outcome'. Eyebrows were raised even among his own press team when Sir Peter spoke openly about what 'Cregan' had done, taking care not to give him a title he did not deserve. He was unequivocal. Cregan had killed the two officers and had been 'protected by a criminal conspiracy to harbour him'. Those who protected him, who considered Cregan and his like 'folk heroes' would be 'brought to book'.

The usual practice when a suspect has been arrested, even one that has been publicly named as a fugitive wanted for double murder, is to take a step back and ensure there can be no accusation from a clever defence barrister that their client has no chance of a fair trial because of prejudicial comments, especially from someone who is a public figure.

Even if the facts are incontrovertible, the form usually is to speak about an alleged crime while taking care never to attribute those crimes to a suspect, except to say there has been an arrest.

But the usual rules went out of the window. These were unique circumstances. And, perhaps more significantly, Sir Peter felt the deaths keenly as a parent.

He has four children around the same ages as Nicola and Fiona.

Others went further. Inspector Ian Hanson, the chairman of the Greater Manchester branch of the Police Federation, the police 'union', told the assembled journalists: "This was cold-blooded murder – the slaughter of the innocent... It's a dark day for policing and it's a dark day for society."

11.

OUR
DARKEST DAY

The nation's media descended on Mottram after the news broke.

Abbey Gardens was cordoned off, and would remain so for two days while scene-of-crime officers sifted through the empty cartridges and grenade fragments strewn all over the street.

Beyond the police tape, Sky News and BBC News 24 set up camp, broadcasting pictures of tearful police colleagues bringing flowers to the scene. Prime Minister David Cameron called the killings a 'despicable act of pure evil'.

Sir Peter Fahy named the two dead officers at a press conference later that day.

He struggled to keep his emotions in check as he told reporters: "Clearly, we are devastated today by the loss of two of our officers... This is one of the darkest days in the history of

Greater Manchester Police, if not of the police service overall because we have lost two deeply loved and valued colleagues, because they are part of our team – policing is very much a family – but also because of the huge efforts that officers have been making to arrest Dale Cregan. The officers involved in that enquiry are shattered by this outcome."

Bruised by the experience of previous failings of his force, he felt the need to defend how his officers had acted even though no-one had asked him to. He made a passionate plea for British police to remain routinely unarmed.

Only two years earlier, Sir Peter had been obliged to apologise to the family of a police marksman who had been shot dead by a colleague during a bungled training drill even though he had not yet taken charge of the force when the incident happened.

An inquest concluded he had been unlawfully killed.

It is one of the many iniquities of Dale Cregan's crimes that he forced decent people to question their own conduct.

Yes, of course there were lessons to be learned, but there had been only one finger on the trigger that morning and it belonged to Cregan.

Sir Peter said: "This has been a huge investigation for us. We have had great support from other forces, from other law enforcement agencies, and we have had some of our best people on this particular investigation. We have carried out over 50 firearm warrants in attempting to locate him. We have made a number of arrests of other people. I think you are aware we have used all forms of publicity, posters and rewards through Crimestoppers to try and locate this man. We believe he has been protected by a criminal conspiracy to harbour him and we are absolutely determined to fully investigate that conspiracy and bring the people involved to book.

"This case tells us something about the nature of organised crime, the web of intimidation it creates and the fact that some people see others as folk heroes for being involved in this kind of activity. We have had officers on armed patrol 24 hours a day, seven days a week in the Clayton and Droylsden area, but clearly we cannot send armed officers to the hundreds of incidents we get, not only in these areas, but also in other areas. These were two officers going about their normal duties.

"Like all officers, they went to a variety of incidents not knowing what it was they would face. Clearly, the police service is not perfect. We know that there have been a number of high-profile incidents but, below that, day-in, day-out police officers go about their duties, going to dangerous situations and unexpected situations while showing great bravery and great courage, and they are with people at the very worst moment in their lives. This is exactly what these two officers were doing.

"Clearly, we are a force who are routinely unarmed, though we have great expertise in our officers in armed support. We are passionate that the British style of policing is routinely unarmed policing. Sadly, we know from experience in America and other countries that have armed officers, it does nothing to stop officers being injured or shot dead.

"We are absolutely devastated by this loss and our thoughts and condolences go out to the officers of these families, their friends and particularly their colleagues who work with them day-in and day-out because they are absolutely shocked and distressed by the events of this morning... Greater Manchester Police is in mourning today. We have lost two very brave and courageous colleagues who exemplified the very best of British policing.

"We are determined to make sure we carry out the fullest investigation into their deaths and bring to justice all those who may be involved in planning these awful events and harbouring those involved."

As news of the police murders went around the globe, GMP officers of all ranks gathered in the canteen at the force HQ. They were stunned and silent. They sat in small groups, barely saying a word to one another. Cregan was now in custody in police cells over the road, also saying virtually nothing.

At about 7pm, a taxi pulled up outside the front entrance.

A man, clearly the worse for drink, stepped out of the cab and staggered over to the front desk. Police officers in the canteen and on guard beside the entrance feared the worst and readied themselves for trouble.

The man said: "I've been in trouble with the law all my life. I fucking hate the police. But what happened today was bang out of order." He pulled out a bouquet of flowers, laid it on the counter, turned on his heels and left.

The brutal murder of two unarmed police officers had clearly shocked at least one member of Manchester's notorious criminal fraternity.

The following day Sir Peter visited the scene and added a wreath to the growing floral tribute in Mottram, standing with colleagues in silence while the rain fell. He paid another tribute to the fallen officers: "These were two wonderful human beings, two very dedicated officers. Two very proud families are obviously devastated by their loss."

Other police colleagues paid their own tribute.

Sgt Tasmin Gray, 42, based at Hyde, worked the shift before C Relief and would routinely speak to the fallen officers during the handover.

She said: "I am just stunned and shocked. There aren't words. We worked quite a lot with the pair. They were lovely. Nicky wasn't even born when I joined the job. I used to look at her and think I was so old. They were two lovely girls. Fiona was a solid officer. She was lovely. They both were. She was one of the first in and was ready to go and relieve my shift. Fiona was looking forward to her wedding. People have known that was happening for a long time. My officers would chat to them during the handover between our shifts. Nicola had only been in the force for three years. She was one of the last student officers to come through. You start to feel old when you see youngsters coming through."

Like the chief constable, she didn't believe that being armed would have made any difference: "It seems they didn't have a chance. It's one of those situations where I don't think anyone could have foreseen this."

Home Secretary Theresa May was regarded as a foe by many police officers for slashing budgets and making drastic changes to policing. Although the vast majority of officers continued to disagree with her ideas, some would change their opinion of her over the subsequent weeks and months, particular those at the heart of the continuing investigation into the criminal conspiracy to protect Dale Cregan.

She insisted on keeping abreast of the investigation as it continued and received monthly updates. It seems she had in mind new legislation to give police more powers to intercept and monitor communications between criminals. Her task was simpler when news broke of the police murders.

She did pretty much all she could at that stage, and that was to express her outrage at the killing. She said: "This is a deeply shocking incident. It is a terrible reminder of the risks that police officers face every day in keeping our communities safe."

Shadow Home Secretary Yvette Cooper laid flowers at the scene and said: "These two brave officers were killed in terrible circumstances."

Police officers were also knocking on doors in Diggle, near Oldham, the Isle of Man, and in Sale to break the tragic news to the families and partners.

The day after the murders, Fiona Bone's father, Paul, and mother, June, gave an interview to their local newspaper, the Isle of Man Gazette. They hadn't sleep that night. In measured terms, Mr Bone called for the death penalty to be reintroduced for anyone who murdered a member of the emergency services while they were on duty.

"We're shocked, just numb," said Mr Bone, who served as an aircraft engineer with the RAF based at Castle Donington in Derbyshire before moving to the Isle of Man in 1997 after landing a job as an engineer with Manx Airlines. "We heard on the news that two police officers had been shot and within three minutes, two policemen were at the door. That's when we heard – at 1.03pm."

He added: "She was calm and collected, nice to be around. We will miss her so much. She loved the job, she lapped it up. When she was put into an office, she hated it. She wanted to go where the action was."

And he made it clear that Cregan deserved to be executed for his crimes: "I believe the death penalty should be imposed for anyone who shoots any uniformed emergency services personnel on duty, whether they are a police officer, paramedic or a firefighter. They put themselves on the line for the public."

Fiona had attended the sixth form at Castle Rushen High School in Port St Mary when the family moved to the Isle of Man.

The flag flew at half mast at the school where headteacher Andrew Cole said that Fiona's 'outgoing nature, friendliness and undaunted sense of humour saw her quickly make new friends' after she joined the sixth form in 1997.

He added: "Fiona was pleasant and courteous and enjoyed good relationships with everyone she came into contact with. Her form tutor noted that she had a great sense of responsibility and was totally reliable. These are no doubt qualities that supported her in being such a good police officer."

The next day Mr and Mrs Bone flew into Manchester, and immediately visited the crime scene in Mottram where their daughter had been murdered. They paused, like so many others, at the expanding row of wreaths which was growing at the top of Abbey Gardens and read some of the messages of sympathy. They would meet with the chief constable later that day.

Police officers also had to knock on a door in Sale, the same one Fiona Bone had left earlier that day in darkness, to inform her partner, Clare Curran, that Fiona was dead.

It was devastating not only for Clare, but also her daughter, Jessie, from a previous relationship, who had grown to love Fiona.

Only that morning the couple had discussed their plans for a civil partnership ceremony."

After they had gathered themselves, Nicola Hughes' dad, Bryn, and mother, Susan, released their own statement.

They said their 'beautiful daughter' had left their home that morning to do 'the job she loved'. The couple, who have a younger son, Sam, said: "Nicola was our only daughter and a beautiful child. She was always happy with life and lived for her family. She had an infectious personality and sense of humour and was a very caring and loving girl. When she left the house this morning, she was going to the job she loved. Nicola always wanted to make a difference and, in doing so, she made such a big difference to everyone she knew. She cared about everyone and especially her colleagues.

"Nicola was only 23 years old and had the whole of her life in front of her. We cannot express how we feel today except to say we have always been exceedingly proud of Nicola and always will be. She knew she was loved by us all and we shall all miss her dreadfully."

Nicola's cousin, Naomi Walker, 24, from Scouthead, Oldham,

said: "Our mums were pregnant at the same time and I have known her all my life. She would do anything for anyone. She honestly could not do enough for you. She used to invite me round for tea and before we went out she'd invite me around to hers to get ready together. She had always wanted to be in the police. It was really hard for her to get in and she had to do lots of training. I'll never forget when she got in. She was thrilled and was texting everyone. She had to do some crazy shifts, but she loved it."

Naomi described Nicola as 'one of the bravest people I know'. She said: "Nicky never really spoke about the dangers of it and she was never scared. She could look after herself, did karate, and she was really brave. Since she became a police officer, she was the happiest I had seen her."

She continued: "It's a shock and it hasn't sunk in yet. I keep seeing Nicky's picture on the TV and I can't believe it. Her brother, Sam, is in bits about it. I think he wants to be a police officer too."

An online book of condolence was opened and soon there were 30,000 messages of support – a good indicator of how appalled the general public were by the deaths.

ACC Garry Shewan said: "Without doubt yesterday was the hardest and most upsetting day of my career. The impact of yesterday's events will be felt by the force, residents of Greater Manchester and most importantly Nicola and Fiona's family, friends and colleagues for many, many years, such was the regard in which they were held. I hope, like me, Nicola and Fiona's family find some comfort in the many thousand s of messages of condolence and support that we have received. The reaction has been overwhelming and I want to publicly thank those who have taken time out to pay tribute to Fiona and Nicola and pass on their kind words of support, love and condolence. Two hardworking and brave young women did not go home to their loved ones as a result of a calculated and malicious plan. We are determined to bring each and every person involved in this incident to justice."

The deaths seemed to bring out the best – and the worst – in humanity.

Officers and well-wishers would run marathons, trek across deserts, cycle the length of the country, organise celebrity football matches and even release a single in memory of the two fallen officers.

Others showed how ugly human nature can be.

On the very day Fiona and Nicola were murdered, Barry Thew, 39, walked through Radcliffe town centre near Bury wearing a t-shirt which read 'one less pig perfect justice' on the front, while on the back was written 'kill a cop 4 fun.com'. Thew, who had a lengthy criminal record, was later jailed for four months plus another four for breaching a suspended prison sentence.

Judge Peter Lakin told him: "This, on any view, is a shocking case. Your response to the shocking events was to parade around in a t-shirt in the centre of Radcliffe which had on it the most disgusting of slogans. In my judgement, it is utterly depressing that you felt able to stoop so low as to behave in that way. Your mindless behaviour has added to the pain of everyone touched by the death of these young officers. You have shown no remorse."

Thew wasn't alone.

Another young man, Jordan Curran, 21, of Sandybrook Drive in Blackley, north Manchester, told police officers he was 'glad' the two officers had been killed as he swore during a confrontation with officers.

He had been helping a woman who had collapsed in the street but when police arrived he couldn't resist having a go. He was later handed a 12-month community order after admitting using threatening behaviour. In another incident, a boy of 16 taunted colleagues of Nicola and Fiona at Ashton-under-Lyne police station, saying he wished they had been stabbed rather than shot 'to make it more painful'. He also shouted words of praise for Dale Cregan. He made the upsetting remarks while he was arrested for having a cosh. He also ended up in court and was handed an 18-month rehabilitation order. Part of the order required him to build a memorial garden for the two murdered officers.

Grief would catch up with officers and families in the most unusual ways and places. Insp Hanson, the chairman of the GMP branch of the Police Federation, had been on a virtually non-stop round of interviews, immediately after the deaths.

At the news conference 24 hours earlier, he had spoken forcefully and frankly and it was no surprise he would be in demand. He had become an eloquent voice speaking up for the rank-and-file over the preceding years and was so again in the days after the officers were murdered.

And he had good reason to be more forthright than usual as he had been Fiona's inspector on the Tameside division before taking up a more active role with 'The Fed', although he never made that public.

He recalled how extremely polite she was as a probationer and how, like all rookie officers, she had fretted about how to complete her 'probationer development profile', a tortuous series of forms every newcomer into GMP must navigate. "Don't worry about it," the inspector had told her. "Don't stress about filling out bloody forms. Just do your best and everything else will slot into place. When you've done your two years' probation, me and you will go round the back of the nick and throw it into the wheelie bin."

It was with a tear in his eye he later noted: "I left before we managed to do that." He described her as 'incredibly well-mannered, very keen and enthusiastic and she got stuck in'. He added: "She just didn't hesitate and that quickly endeared her to colleagues on her shift. Despite her size, she backed people up and got stuck in."

None of Insp Hanson's personal recollections were offered during a series of TV interviews he conducted that day, among them a spiky exchange with Jeremy Paxman on Newsnight who questioned police efforts on gun crime.

Paxman was told it 'wasn't the time' for that particular debate. Hanson was sitting in the canteen at the BBC when he was asked to compose a press release for the Police Federation nationally. As he drafted it on his iPad, he burst into tears. Perhaps luckily, no-one saw him.

He had understood intellectually that two colleagues had been murdered. But it was only while writing that press release he understood it emotionally.

Many months later, in an interview in his office in Reddish, it was clear he was still struggling to come to terms with the deaths.

He suffered no such frailty when summing up what he thought of Cregan: "I want him to die in prison. I want him to spend the rest of his miserable life thinking about the life he could have had. He wanted to be the big man. He's very quickly going to be nothing more than a number and in a very short period of time, people in Greater Manchester won't even know who Dale Cregan was. And when he dies in prison many years from now, nobody will even care. I would contrast that with the names of Fiona Bone and Nicola Hughes who will forever epitomise what's good about Greater Manchester Police and Greater Manchester. That will never be forgotten."

As officers all across GMP struggled to come to terms with the murder of two of their colleagues, an aide at Downing Street rang the police station at Ashton-under-Lyne. He informed officers about 'what Dave would like to do'.

The Prime Minister David Cameron had wanted to speak to members of C Relief, and other 999 workers who went to the scene at Abbey Gardens, to offer them his personal condolences and support. The aide must have been rather taken aback when he was told: "Let me stop you right there."

He was left in no doubt that this wasn't 'Dave's gig' and it would be up to the officers on C Relief whether they wanted to meet the Prime Minister or not.

AMBUSH

The next couple of hours must have been rather uncomfortable at Downing Street, where the aide in question must have at least considered the possibility that the most important man in the country was about to be snubbed by the coppers of C Relief.

It wouldn't have mattered which shift was canvassed anywhere across GMP.

The coalition was almost universally loathed among the rank-and-file for the police cuts and changes to the service. Only four months earlier some 30,000 bobbies from Manchester and around the country had marched on Westminster to give vent to their anger at budget cuts, reduced pensions and changes to terms and conditions that many viewed as a vindictive attack on the police. Why would they now want to shake hands with one of the principle architects of hated police reform? In the end, hostilities were put aside and the request was treated for what it was – a real attempt to reach out and show support.

The reaction to the suggestion was 'mixed', according to insiders, but Downing Street was called back and assured 'Dave' would be welcome. The following day, Mr Cameron met the officers of C Relief and other emergency workers, for instance the paramedics who treated Nicola Hughes at the scene.

The meeting didn't happen at a police station. Instead, it happened in a room at LA Fitness in Hyde. There were no cameras, no journalists. So those present knew it wasn't a publicity stunt, and no news of the event leaked out to the press. "He was in a difficult position. It can't have been easy for him. But he said the right things," said one who was at the meeting.

OUR DARKEST DAY

The gathering had been organised for more than just meeting the Prime Minister. It had also been an opportunity for police officers to discuss informally the trauma they had collectively experienced away from the pressure of work and away from the nick.

When the moment came for the meet-and-greet with the PM, three of the officers quietly made themselves scarce. They moved over to the bar area while Mr Cameron was speaking to the officers.

For them at least, no charm or sympathy, however genuinely expressed, could make them forget the cost-cutting programme which had seen hundreds of their colleagues leave GMP.

But there were more important things to worry about at that moment in time.

As detectives slowly started piecing together the sequence of events – starting back at the Cotton Tree in May – the rest of GMP prepared for one of the worst couple of days in its history.

It was time to bury two of their own, and two of their absolute best.

12.

FAREWELL

October 3, 2012

A thin blue line stretched up either side of Deansgate as far as the eye could see. Manchester's main thoroughfare was silent, save for the sound of the wind.

Police officers had come to pay their respects and – standing proudly and quietly in their uniforms – they were shoulder to shoulder on the pavement. Many had tears in their eyes. All had a lump in their throat.

Their uniforms bore insignias from constabularies from all around the country: Cheshire, North Wales, Essex, Sussex, Warwickshire, West Midlands, the Metropolitan police and more. Just behind them stood ordinary members of the public – office workers who had left their desks, shop workers who abandoned their tills and many more who just wanted to show their support.

AMBUSH

Silence.

Then a small ripple of applause, growing ever louder, as the cortege carrying the body of PC Nicola Hughes turned into Deansgate, headed by six mounted police officers in full ceremonial dress.

Her body moved up Deansgate, inch by inch.

Some threw flowers onto the hearse. Moments later, the bells in the tower of Manchester Cathedral began to toll. As the cortege passed them, those who had lined Deansgate turned and followed as it headed towards the cathedral.

Inside one of the following limousines, Nicola Hughes' heartbroken father, Bryn, looked through the window and saw for himself those who had come to say farewell to his daughter, some with heads bowed and others clapping.

He was bursting both with pride and indescribable sadness. Later, he recalled: "It was surreal. When we got to Deansgate, it looked a huge, dark tunnel, there were that many people. You had that mixture of being really proud and sorrow at the same time."

Colleagues from C Relief carried Nicola's coffin, draped with a wreath of white roses, her gloves and police hat, into the church. A thousand mourners filled the pews, among them the chief constables of all 43 police forces in England and Wales. Conspicuously absent were the Prime Minister or any leading politicians. It wasn't meant as a snub. But this was a day for the 'police family' to come together. Outside the church, mourners who couldn't get in watched the service on a large screen in Cathedral Gardens.

FAREWELL

"We will never forget her great sacrifice," said her chief constable, Sir Peter Fahy, one of many who paid heart-felt and moving tributes.

The following day, it was time to say farewell to Fiona Bone. And Manchester paused again.

This time, bagpipes played as Fiona's coffin was carried into the cathedral to reflect her Scottish roots. Her partner Clare's five-year-old daughter, Jessie, wore a pink dress and carried a wand as she walked into the cathedral's second police funeral in two days. Manchester United manager, Sir Alex Ferguson, was among the mourners. To reflect the family's wishes, only audio of the service was beamed into Cathedral Gardens. Sir Peter and many of the same officers who had paid tribute the day before, did so again. Later, Fiona's father, Paul, would express his gratitude: "We are ever so grateful to the people of Manchester and all those police who came up to the funeral, it wasn't a funeral I had ever experienced before, it was like a state occasion."

At the beginning of the same week, a very different funeral had taken place in Clayton as David Short – Cregan's hated nemesis – was also laid to rest.

On the morning of the service, someone daubed the walls of St Willibrord's RC church with the words: "Dale Cregan is a God."

Council officials quickly covered the graffiti and cleaned it away before the service began.

Fearing trouble, police mounted a huge security operation around the church. The police helicopter, India 99, kept a close eye on proceedings from the air. Police officers were stationed on street corners but kept their distance for fear of inflaming emotions. As part of the security operation, police had successfully applied to magistrates to close all 27 pubs in Droylsden for the day.

Short's funeral cortege began outside his home on Folkestone Road East before making its way to the church less than a mile away. His hearse, adorned with floral tributes including messages such as 'Grandad' and 'Dad', led the way followed by a horse-drawn carriage carrying his coffin.

The horses were draped in Manchester City flags. A crowd of several hundred gathered on the streets before following the family.

They may have come from very different backgrounds, but the Short, the Bone and Hughes families shared one thing in common: their lives had been blown apart by the same man and when the trial started, they sat together in the public gallery, if not shoulder to shoulder, then at least united in grief.

The demands of the modern media machine eventually prompted the Bone and Hughes families to again pay tribute to their respective daughters, if for nothing else than to attempt to draw some sort of a line under the very public nature of their ordeals.

They would talk only once and only on the understanding they would not be doorstepped by the media.

Nicola's father, Bryn, sometimes tearful and occasionally laughing about memories of his beloved daughter, described the tragedy as a 'nightmare you cannot wake from'.

FAREWELL

The prison officer was told of his daughter's murder by a police officer who was waiting outside his house when he returned home from work. Bereft, he rang his wife and sobbed: "She's dead."

He feared for his daughter, as any parent would, when she joined the police, but he knew she was sensible. She may only have been small, but she could handle herself.

Like her dad, who ran Karate Club Oldham Kyokushinkai, she had been passionate about karate since the age of 10 and was a green belt. The little fighter also had a warm heart, trying her best to welcome her father's new wife, Natalie, into the family.

Bryn and Natalie, 32, both prison officers, held hands as they sat on a sofa and paid tribute to Nicola during an interview at GMP's Sedgeley Park complex, north of Manchester.

While they were willing to talk about Nicola, they didn't want to dignify Cregan by commenting on him, his crime or what punishment he deserved. Instead, they concentrated on Nicola's life, rather than how she met her death.

Nicola went to Saddleworth School and then Oldham Sixth Form College where she did A-levels in psychology and law. After leaving, she went to Huddersfield University where she studied social sciences and psychology, but she abandoned the degree halfway through her first year.

She told her father: "This isn't for me." She applied and joined GMP, aged 20. Nicola was a busy, productive girl – she held down part-time jobs at a shoe shop and at the Bull's Head pub in Delph, waiting-on in the tapas restaurant there. Outside work, she liked 'make-up, nails, hair dye and studying'.

AMBUSH

When she realised her dream of joining the police, Nicola was thrilled. "She was so excited when she showed us her warrant card for the first time," said Natalie. Bryn continued: "She was as happy as anything. She was interested in forensic psychology and read a lot on it and watched it on the television. She wanted to find something interesting, something challenging and something long-term secure."

Nicola was motivated by public spirit, according to Natalie, and wanted a job where she would 'make a difference, to help people'.

Bryn smiled and occasionally laughed as he explained how his daughter's sense of public spirit would often envelop him, even when his inclination was rather different.

He said: "She just wanted to help people from an early age. I remember she used to check on an elderly neighbour and the next thing she said 'you need to go round to fix her windows'. She was always volunteering me for things. She must have thought I had the same inclination to volunteer and help people. She didn't go in for any official volunteering or anything like that. She didn't do all that. It was for friends and neighbours and relations. She really wanted to help them. If she couldn't help them, she would volunteer me! Once there was a school cycling trip and she checked my diary to see if I was off. I ended up cycling 26 miles. On another occasion all her class were going swimming and they needed some help. She spoke to the head teacher and told him 'my dad can do that'. I didn't know I was going to be looking after 26 boys on the trip, all because Nicola volunteered me. I had no choice. That's the way she put it."

FAREWELL

Natalie said: "She could always get you to do whatever she wanted. We were all really, really proud (when she joined the police). She really wanted it. You know underneath it's a dangerous job, but you don't think about that. You see she's enjoying herself and her job... She wasn't just proud. She loved her job. I can't think of anybody who loved her job that much. She was driven, and if she wanted something, she would go out and get it."

Of course, when Nicola joined the force, there were unspoken worries about the dangers she would face, although these fears were pushed to the back of minds as she was such a combative, practical and sensible young woman.

Natalie explained: "You don't think about it that much. There's a brief acknowledgment that it's a dangerous job she's doing. You just don't think something like that will happen to your family or begin to think about it."

"You know it's dangerous, that they are dealing with dangerous people," said Bryn. "But it wasn't every day you were thinking 'I hope she's alright'. Obviously, when she spoke about things, about what she did last night and this or that happened, you think hmmmmm. But you knew she would be sensible."

It was when asked how they found out about Nicola's murder that Bryn struggled to keep his composure.

On his way home from work, he had received a call from a detective on his mobile as he drove. The officer said he was waiting for him at his home and when Bryn asked if it was about Nicola, the officer didn't answer. Bryn realised it was something serious about his daughter. When he got home, he was told the devastating news.

"I was driving home from work. I got a call from a DCI..." said Bryn, whose eyes filled with tears. His wife comforted him and took over: "Bryn had just had an interview for a new job at work. He was driving home and the police contacted him and said they were at his house and they were waiting to speak to him. They didn't tell him initially what happened, but he put two and two together and he knew something quite serious had happened to Nicola. Eventually we found out she had been killed. He drove the rest of the way home and the police were there at the house. He rang me at work to tell me what had happened. I just remember him saying 'Natalie, Nicola's dead'. You are just in shock. Your head is spinning."

Having regained his composure, Bryn continued: "It was disbelief. It's a nightmare you can't wake up from. It's a horror film you are watching on television. You want to pause and rewind, as you know what's coming, but you can't."

"It's just constant disbelief," said Natalie. "It just keeps hitting you all over again that it's real. It just affects your whole life in ways you just cannot imagine. It makes you realise your own mortality. It makes you think that it could be anybody at any time, things you have never really thought of before."

They agreed what had sustained them was the well-wishers, flowers and support from both in and out of the police. "It's been overwhelming," said Bryn. "There's obviously been a great deal of sympathy and shock. GMP couldn't do enough." Natalie went further: "If we had not had that kind of support from the police in the very early days, we could not have kept going. We didn't know what way was up. We were kind of just there for the first few weeks, but we weren't really there. We were just like zombies."

They spoke about the 'thousands' of cards they received from well-wishers, including one which featured a photo of a double rainbow over Hyde taken on the day the two officers were killed. "People had just been emotionally touched by what had happened," said Natalie.

Despite their grief, the pair hoped Nicola's death would not be in vain and that, perhaps, it would encourage greater respect towards police from a sometimes cynical public.

"I don't know what GMP was like beforehand, but if this has brought people together and made people respect the police more, then I think that would be a fitting legacy," said Bryn.

A week after their interview, it was the turn of the father and sister of Fiona Bone. It took place at GMP's HQ at Central Park. It was fitting for her ex-serviceman father, Paul, 64, that there were no histrionics, no outbursts. Just a calm and measured summary of the awful predicament in which his family had found itself. He was the epitome of the British stiff upper lip. Again, the interview was an attempt to draw a line under matters. They would speak just once and attempt to get on with their lives.

Describing his daughter's character and how they tried hard to keep in touch, despite their jobs, Paul said: "She was a lovely person really, easy to get on with, fairly active, she wanted to help people and enjoyed life, mostly. Because we worked such odd hours – I was working as a line maintenance controller, which was a 24-hour job, and she was working more or less a

24-hour job – we used to ring each other on the way to work and back, so we used to speak three, four, five times a week. We used to have a very good relationship, no real arguments. We used to enjoy coming over to Manchester to see her...helping her move house... I was in the airforce so we moved around the country a lot. She was born in Norwich (and) we got posted up to Lossiemouth. She was born on 31st December 1979 and from there we went to Bruggen for three years in Germany, then we went back to Lossiemouth, first time on 12 Squadron, second time 208 Squadron. That's why she liked to claim she was Scottish. If you really wanted to annoy her, you told her she 'was English because you were born in Norwich'."

Fiona appeared to protect her father from the more gruesome details of policing. He only got 'edited highlights' and she gave the impression nothing dangerous was ever happening. Even when she was commended for a burglary and robbery investigation, Fiona never mentioned it to her dad.

Paul said: "We didn't actually get told about that. That was obviously one of the things she didn't want us to know about. We only found out after she died."

Fiona did tell Vicky but, modest as ever, said it was a team effort. "She just played it down really," said Vicky. Dad continued: "I was happy if she was happy; it was her life. I mean most policemen don't die, let's face it. It's the very odd one that does."

Fiona did tell her family about the first sudden death she had to deal with.

She had to roll over the body of an elderly man to check for stab wounds. There were none. Paul described another incident his daughter came across while out on patrol: "She was driving along and was the first officer on the scene of a motorcycle accident and the motorcyclist was dead. I think it was the first death she had ever experienced," he said.

"She got a bit upset about that. Usually it was just the nice stories we got told, like when she was on her driving test and ended up doing a car chase. She was on the police driving test to get her first license to drive a police panda car and started chasing a car with smoke coming out of the boot."

He described how Fiona had been planning to adopt her partner Clare Curran's daughter from a previous relationship, Jessie. Fiona and the little girl were very close. In fact, the three girls would often visit Paul in the Isle of Man: "They used to come across when Fiona got days off if it coincided with holidays or school holidays. They would come across for three or four days or a week and we would go across a couple of times, two or three times a year."

Her wedding plans were well advanced. Fiona and Clare were 'very switched on' and had 'got it nailed' when it came to the details, according to Vicky.

Paul advised the couple to get cracking rather than have a long engagement.

In fact, the date of the ceremony would have been just a few days after the interview.

In love, in a good job, and about to get hitched, Paul agreed Fiona was the happiest she had ever been: "Yep. She was really happy with herself and with what was going on in her life."

Vicky concurred: "Yes it was. She was so excited about getting married."

Paul insisted he wasn't angry his daughter's life had been cut short in its prime. He explained: "Angry is not really the right word, numb might be. Yeah, numb." The last time he saw 'the girls' was when they came over to the island at Easter. He spoke on the phone with Fiona just a few days before she was killed. It was just a 'routine' chat. Paul and his wife, June, were at home when they saw a news item about two officers being killed or injured.

"We saw a quick glimpse on the BBC 1 O'Clock news, that two people, two policemen had been killed and I hate to say it, within 30 seconds of it being on the TV, there was a knock at the door with two policemen at the door," said Paul. "They told us unfortunately our daughter was one of the two policewomen that had been killed. I think the TV had said two had been injured, not two killed... We were both totally shocked really, couldn't believe it. We invited the policemen to have a cup of tea, they said they were waiting for other policemen to come from Douglas with more details because they didn't really know much more other than they had to come and tell us our daughter had been killed."

The days that followed were 'a blur'. Paul said: "The next day we were flown out into Manchester and then we went to a continuous number of briefings and what's going on, how it happened and inquests, things for about a week. We didn't really have much time to think or stop."

The Bone family tried not to read the newspapers or watch

the news. It would have been too painful. It also meant that, at first, they weren't aware of the huge outpouring of public sympathy.

Paul explained: "We were told there was a lot of public outpourings. We didn't really have the TV on and we didn't read the newspapers. The first time we knew how it had affected ordinary policemen was when we went to the coroners' court and the policemen that were guarding the court wanted to hug and shake hands and generally not act like policemen act. We had met, by that stage, her shift so we knew they were affected but you expect them to be affected because they were part of her team but the people there were not part of her team, they were upset as well."

Paul said he didn't think about Dale Cregan: "He lives in a different world and planet to me, from what we have heard and read of the court case. He's just got a totally different mindset. I can't imagine anyone thinking, 'I'm going to shoot a policeman today because they have upset me'. If everyone thought like that speed cameras and police officers would be in real trouble."

The crime underworld inhabited by Cregan and others was a world away from the largely peaceful and rural locations the Bone family had been used to.

Paul said: "I'm not saying being in a military family gives you an isolated life, but airforce stations, most geographic locations are out in the country and very peaceful. Fiona was paranoid about locking her front door. We can leave it unlocked for weeks and no one would notice. No one cares on the Isle of Man. You just don't think about crime like people in the mainland think about it."

Paul repeated a call for the return of the death penalty.

At the time he explained his reasoning in measured terms: "I believe the death penalty should be imposed for anyone who shoots any uniformed emergency services personnel on duty, whether they are a police officer, paramedic or a firefighter. They put themselves on the line for the public.

"One of the problems is when they did away with hanging, in the '60s, we were told life would mean life; now it's very flexible, or life is a very flexible sentence. Alright, (Home Secretary) Theresa May has said life for killing a policeman. It should extend to all uniformed public servants."

He backed capital punishment in certain circumstances and Cregan was 'possibly' a candidate. Asked if he would hang Cregan, he said: "As long as I didn't have to do it – it's the coward's way out."

Vicky wondered whether Cregan would have embarked on his murder spree if capital punishment still existed, although Paul questioned whether a jury would be more reluctant to convict and even suggested capital punishment would be more cost-effective than keeping serious criminals behind bars for decade after decade. He said: "When they are cutting back on everything else, prisoners costing thousands to keep in jail, 30 to 40 years, it's an awfully long time."

Paul was typically phlegmatic when asked how he was coping: "I would've preferred not to lose her, but people die. Being ex-military, people died in the military. You are just used to it. You just hope it is not one of yours. You just have to live with it." His wife, June, was struggling but 'getting better', he said.

FAREWELL

Asked about their abiding memory of Fiona, Paul offered two contrasting images of his daughter: "Fiona with a glass of wine! And the only thing we ever fell out over, driving – she was a terrible driver! People who knew Fiona will remember Fiona the right way. We had a letter after she died from people she had helped or assisted. They were absolutely heartbroken she died because she was so helpful."

Vicky painted a third picture of Fiona: "Just giggling and just having a laugh and just being sisters. The last time the two of us were on the phone, we were giggling away, just being silly, talking about her wedding."

The grief, dashed hopes and sense of loss being felt by parents, siblings, partners and colleagues of the slain officers, was almost too painful to endure.

13.

WOUNDS THAT RUN DEEP

Six months after two of his officers had been murdered, Chief Supt Nick Adderley was in reflective mood in his office at Ashton-under-Lyne Police Station.

He spoke openly about how he and his officers found out about the deaths of two loved colleagues back on the morning of September 18; how they were powerless to do anything as they heard each detail broadcast over the police airwaves.

He had served as a lieutenant with the Royal Navy for 10 years. He had seen colleagues die in the Falklands conflict. But this was different, somehow harder to take.

Cregan's rules of engagement were not from any battlefield he had known.

Cregan had been an utter coward.

Fiona and Nicola were unarmed and caught by surprise,

like all his victims. But there was something more pernicious gnawing away at the insides of the senior police officer: self-doubt and a sense of guilt.

As the commander of the Tameside sub-division of GMP, Chief Supt Adderley felt somehow responsible for the deaths of his own officers. Not only that, but he also felt a fraud as a senior officer for daring to suggest – albeit only implicitly – that he could protect the public when he couldn't even protect his own officers. And what made it harder still for an ex-serviceman and a man of action, a man who every day of his working life was making important decisions, was the manner in which he had learned about the deaths. He had been powerless to do anything.

Remembering the raw details from that day is an ordeal for Adderley.

"I remember it was a Tuesday and every Tuesday we have a senior leadership team meeting at Ashton," said the officer, matter-of-factly. "We were sitting there discussing various things about the threats to life around the murders of two Short family members. The mood was generally light-hearted. It was at around 11am there was a bang on the door and the door of the conference room burst open. A detective sergeant came in and said something was happening at Hyde, and Cregan had handed himself in. We all went into my office and I switched on my police radio, and as soon as it came on, it burst into life. It was absolute bedlam. Then my mobile started going. It was an assistant chief constable. Then the landline rang. It was the chief constable. And at the same time I'm trying to listen to the radio. It was fairly chaotic. We were trying to make sense of what was going on and get confirmation it was Cregan.

"In the meantime, I can hear the control room operator saying we had a patrol at Abbey Gardens and there had been gunshots and he'd try to raise them. The control room was trying to contact them and repeating their call-sign. In the meantime we were hearing Cregan had said he had 'done two officers'. I sent a senior officer down to Hyde as there was a murder suspect at the police station. Obviously, we were worried that the vehicle he had arrived in was rigged to explode and that there might be hand grenades in it. We were struggling to get real confirmation of what was going on.

"As a senior officer, it's a really difficult balancing act you have to perform. You want information from people at the scene but you don't want to interfere because they have a lot to do. There came a point where we had two officers who weren't answering their call-sign. It was fairly obvious something wasn't right. I got onto the radio and asked for the duty inspector at Hyde to contact me. In the meantime, another patrol arrived at Abbey Gardens and they were relaying information to the duty inspector. By the time I got hold of him he was already there at Abbey Gardens. He said Fiona was already dead and they were working on Nicola.

"I was in the armed forces and experienced loss of life in active service, but this was completely different. It might be viewed as sexist, but does the fact they were female make any difference? Yes, it does. The big thing for me was the rules of engagement here were completely different.

"They were ambushed."

Pointing across the room, he continued: "I was stood over that desk there. I was on that phone. I remember my mobile going off and just ignoring it and I remember the radio being chaotic. It was like an out-of-body experience. It was like you weren't really there. All the military training I've had and all the police training I've had can never ever prepare you for something like that. You always have a plan. There's always options; always something you can do, and suddenly you realise there's absolutely nothing you can do here.

"The first consideration was Cregan. You have to click into operational mode. Cregan was in custody and secure. We had one officer dead at Abbey Gardens and one likely to die and being worked on. There were a lot of distressed people looking at you really for direction. The whole experience was just odd. An assistant chief constable was sent over to help with the welfare of the officers here on this division. And we had to contact next of kin."

As he spoke, his calm demeanour was at odds with the turmoil his words described, and when asked how he felt, it was clear that the deaths of the two officers had severely affected him.

He said: "At the time, I felt physically sick. That sick feeling. I could have been physically sick. That lasted for a few days afterwards. After a time that feeling of sickness subsided. I'm not going to say guilt. It's more than guilt. It's a feeling of responsibility. In some respects you feel a bit of a fraud now because every day you are out there to the public saying 'we will keep you safe' and 'tell us what's going on' and 'we will sort it out' and 'we will look after you' and yet you have failed miserably in looking after your own people.

"That legitimacy is still an issue with me.

"No matter how much we, as a service, look at crewing policies and the safeguards and everything else, you still feel as though you are a bit of a fraud now. I know that's just emotional nonsense. I know that. But you can't help feeling the way that you feel. Even now I can't think of what I could have done differently based on the information we had at the time."

He spoke compassionately about the officers who followed PCs Hughes and Bone into Abbey Gardens to find their colleagues dead or dying: "They're not good. The reality is that neither of those two are ever likely to return to frontline duties again. They continue to be supported by us and by the force.

"We are looking at how to support one of them out of the organisation. The other one was only a matter of weeks away (from returning to work) before they decided they couldn't do it. Both those officers I know very well. They're really, really good hard-working officers. One of them said to me about six weeks ago that they desperately needed to get back to work, but they can't return to Tameside. We made arrangements for him to work somewhere else, somewhere of his choice. He wanted to get back to work and back into the swing of things.

"But as soon as he put his uniform on, that was it. He fell to pieces saying 'I can't do it again'."

The second officer who had arrived at the scene, a woman, remained traumatised by the terrible injuries she saw on the body of Nicola Hughes when a paramedic pulled away her body armour. A third officer also struggled with the simple act of donning their uniform. "This is the kind of trauma people are still suffering from," said the officer.

In the days after the murders, newspaper reports carried quotes from unnamed residents saying they had seen Cregan but they had been too scared to tell the police.

They claimed that they would be dead before they could spend the £50,000 reward on offer.

One man told the MEN: "I saw him in the pub three or four weeks ago. He had one drink and met a few guys. I did not tell the police because I was too scared."

The so-called wall of silence was not something Chief Supt Adderley recognised: "It just doesn't exist. The community just didn't know. If any of this information had become known to the residents, I have every confidence they would have told us. There just wasn't a wall of silence. All sorts of information was coming in. I remember one elderly gentleman telling us if he saw him, he would tell us straight away, and he didn't even want the £50,000 reward. There was a real desire at work to find this person. It wasn't the wall of silence that was portrayed. All that stuff that you wouldn't have time to spend the £50,000 before you were found and killed. That certainly wasn't the experience I had when I was out there talking to people.

"I would describe the communities of Mottram and Hyde as almost apologetic. They are my words but they came across as apologetic, that they could and should have done more. But there was absolutely nothing they could have done more to help us in any way. What's important now is that

WOUNDS THAT RUN DEEP

this is used as a springboard to build on those links in the community even more and make them more solid than they already are."

The wounds inflicted on the communities of Mottram, Hyde and Clayton by Dale Cregan run deep, and for some they may never recover.

JUSTICE

14.

BAD, NOT MAD

Now that Cregan was finally in custody, GMP began their investigations into a man who had tried his best to tear the police service to pieces.

Growing up, Cregan was an undistinguished pupil at Littlemoss High School in Droylsden.

One former teacher, Gary Robinson, told one national newspaper that Cregan had never impressed in the classroom.

He said: "He was not particularly bright but I knew nothing that indicated that he would have turned into a gangster."

He was small for his age and far from academic. He would grow to a relatively modest 5ft 10in. He soon bulked up with the aid of steroids and regular visits to the gym.

Despite his relatively diminutive stature, he turned himself into a fearsome, physical specimen. He was particularly noted for his enormous thighs. He never shied away from a street fight and was considered something of a local folk hero for standing up to the 'bully' nephews of David Short.

If his academic work wasn't up to much, what set him apart was his drug dealing.

He was buying and selling cannabis from his teenage years. When he left school, he worked as a roofer for a while but soon found the drug business more to his liking. He moved on to dealing in cocaine he sourced from Holland. At his peak, he was raking in £20,000 a week, according to his own estimate.

He was careful, though. The 17 criminal convictions he had amassed, mostly for physical violence, were dwarfed by many of Manchester's more prolific and dangerous offenders.

In 2000, aged 16, he was handed a six-month detention and training order for shoving a pint glass up a victim's backside and twisting it.

That was the only spell Cregan spent behind bars ahead of his murder spree although someone who revelled in the nicknames 'The Animal' and 'The Lunatic' was clearly a man capable of spreading fear.

Despite Cregan's criminal connections, he made sure he only ever sold coke to people he knew. He might not have been academic but he was clever enough to stay under the radar of the police for the most part.

His flourishing drugs business enabled him to drive a Mercedes ML Jeep, a high-powered Range Rover and enjoy a jet-set lifestyle.

There were trips to Amsterdam, Tenerife, France and Thailand, often traveling business class.

With his Armani trainers and t-shirts, and a Rolex on his wrist, Cregan considered himself to be a success story.

Knocking around in Droylsden, the young Cregan had earned himself a reputation as a lad who could handle himself in a scrap.

The beat bobbies who had cause to speak to the young Cregan didn't regard him as a really serious criminal. Although he was a 'gobshite', he was someone with whom they believed they could at least have some form of dialogue. There were other local ne'er-do-wells who they considered beyond their reach.

He wasn't one of those.

Friends described him as sociable, although unpredictable with a few beers down him. Without drawing attention to himself, Cregan quietly became one of Britain's most dangerous criminals.

He was brought up by his mother, Anita, after his father had left the scene when he was still very young.

He was known as a mummy's boy and was always well turned out.

Anita, his brother Dean, sisters Stacey and Kelly all stood by him when he murdered both Mark and David Short, who the Cregans regarded as the enemy just like the Atkinsons did.

They didn't just stand by him. They looked up to him for making a stand against the Shorts and they continued to stand by him even when he killed the two police officers.

They believed he had been forced into a corner by the police. One good friend of the Cregan family, who asked not to be named, said: "I've known them all my life. The reason why

Dale lost the plot and actually killed them police officers was because of the way the police were treating his family. They went round to his sister's house and knifed the ceiling to try to find stuff. They were going to his mum's constantly in front of the kids and grandkids, getting them out at gunpoint and making them lay down when they were naked with just their boxers on. Dale's mum has made a record of everything they did.

The friend continued: "I'm not condoning what Dale did, but what I'm saying is there's two sides to every story. What's made Dale go mental? As soon as he did that, everybody said he hadn't done it, because there's another side to him that everyone sees. Everyone on the estate says 'Dale couldn't have done that, something's wrong'. We know it isn't wrong. We know he did it. But that's what people are saying.

"He's lived in Droylsden his entire life. He's a nice, genuine guy. If you saw him in the pub, you could have a laugh and a drink with him. He's a decent guy. All he's done is protect his family. David Short would have killed his family, I guarantee it. He's an evil, evil man. Dale was protecting his family. We've all discussed it and if David Short was doing that to you, you would do the same. You would have had to because he would have killed your kids. The Shorts have always had trouble with us in Droylsden."

There will be very many people who just don't recognise this description of Cregan, among them the police and the families of all his victims.

Perverse as it seems, it was clear his friends stood by Cregan despite his awful crimes, even though they struggled to understand why he took the lives of two unarmed female police officers.

The experts sent into his cell to pick his brains – doctors Caroline Logan and James Collins – came away with reams of notes, but were really no closer to understanding what made him tick.

All they knew for sure was a brain scan had shown nothing untoward and he certainly wasn't the insane gunman he tried in vain to depict. Between them, the doctors spent more than 15 hours assessing Cregan at the prison, using psychometric tests and interviews.

On their first visit on December 28, 2012, Cregan refused to speak, let alone leave his cell. He wanted to speak to his solicitor first.

When he was visited again in the new year, he decided he would at least talk about his crimes.

Whether or not he had decided to spice up his story to encourage his inquisitors he was sick or crazy, his version of events was certainly startling. Yes, despite the not guilty pleas, he admitted he had slaughtered Mark and David Short and PCs Fiona Bone and Nicola Hughes.

He claimed to have fantasised about killing David Short for the previous five years. When he had shot dead Mark Short in the Cotton Tree, his real target had been the older Short, David.

When he finally got round to killing David Short, Cregan wished he had taken the time to chop his victim's head, arms and legs off rather than simply shoot him and blow up his body with a grenade.

During those hours of interviews in the segregation wing at Strangeways – where Cregan was kept alongside sex offenders and other high-risk inmates – he was keen to give the impression he was unhinged and had acted alone, perhaps to spare his partners in crime so they would be around to protect his family from the Shorts.

It was only when the discussion ventured into more personal areas that he clammed up.

He was reluctant to talk about his childhood and sexuality.

He made out it was because he was shy, but his inquisitors thought this was probably an act.

The first proper interview happened at Strangeways on January 7, 2013, and lasted two hours.

Many more would take place over the coming weeks in which Cregan detailed his violent animosity towards the Shorts, and David Short in particular.

The value of these interviews was at the very least questionable because of the circumstances in which they occurred. Here was a man who wanted to demonstrate that he was crazy and so would be likely to try to say anything to create the image of a disturbed killer who needed treatment rather than punishment.

Whether or not he lied, these interviews nevertheless represent the only time he spoke openly to anyone in authority about his crimes.

He barely said a word through hours and hours of police interviews and decided, after flirting with the idea for weeks, he would not get on the witness stand to tell his story during the trial.

The prison interviews, therefore, were the only insight into what he was thinking.

He told his prison cell visitors he had a 'bad fetish for knives' and his interest in guns came later after spending a couple of years in Tenerife where he visited his sister. Guns became part of his life but Cregan insisted it was more of an obsessive hobby than a necessity for a drug dealer out to protect himself and his interests. He liked to collect them. "I got guns because I loved them," he said.

Once his interest in guns had been awakened, he added a few 'big ones' to his collection – an AK47 and an Uzi. He could not risk keeping them at his mother's house so stashed them elsewhere. Initially he carried the weapons 'all the time' but not so much when he got older. "I got bored with them. I don't like them as much as knives. It's too easy to use them. You just shoot away. I shot David Short in the head three times. I would have preferred it if I had used a knife," Cregan said matter-of-factly to the experts in his cell.

Cregan's fixation with knives included skinning the rabbits he caught on his frequent hunting trips where, armed with a rifle and a hawk, he learned the thrill of the chase.

He told them he was a careful drug dealer; he would only deal cocaine 'with a couple of people I know'. He had been dealing cocaine since his early 20s and had sourced his drugs from England and, later, Holland. Holland was also where he got his grenades, he said.

JUSTICE

For the senior detective who led the investigation into the police murders, Cregan was no folk hero but a narcissist and a coward who murdered them simply to enhance his reputation behind bars for the long jail stretch he knew was coming.

If he was going to Strangeways, he wanted to be top dog in Strangeways.

Greater Manchester Police used several of its most experienced detectives to lead the different parts of the investigation.

The job of leading the inquiry into the murders of the two PCs – dubbed Operation Redwing – was given to Detective Superintendent Simon Barraclough.

At the time, he could have been forgiven for asking someone else to take the reins as – aside from being considered by most as GMP's best detective – he was, perhaps, also the busiest.

A huge, bearded bear of a man, he was already in charge of a mammoth investigation into the saboteur at Stockport's Stepping Hill Hospital, who had poisoned 22 patients in June and July of 2011, killing three of them.

That investigation mushroomed to such an extent it became even bigger than the GMP enquiry into the mass murdering GP Harold Shipman.

No matter how busy he was, GMP's hierarchy wanted their top man on it and that man was Simon Barraclough.

For him, it was about ensuring the investigation was the best it could be regardless of the fact that Cregan had confessed.

He and his team owed that to their two fallen colleagues. His style as a detective was characterised by calm intelligence with a touch of theatre. Just days before the trial got going at Preston

Crown Court, he and other officers held a pre-trial briefing at GMP's HQ at Central Park, north of Manchester city centre.

While the atmosphere was business-like and informal when his colleagues spoke, there was complete silence as he delivered a shocking and unfaltering blow-by-blow account of how the two officers had met their deaths in Abbey Gardens.

You could have heard a pin drop.

He commanded the full and undivided attention of every journalist in that room, as much for the authority of his delivery as for the shocking nature of each awful detail.

The nature of the deaths, and Cregan's choice of weapons, ensured that the public remained transfixed with the case.

How did a Manchester villain procure guns of such deadly persuasion?

And how on earth had he managed to get his hand on the grenades that provoked such terror and appalling injuries?

15.

GUNS AND GRENADES

When Yugoslavia began to disintegrate during the early 1990s, many of the guns used by the old Yugoslav army fell into criminal hands and found their way across Europe and into the clutches of gangsters in England.

It wasn't just guns though.

Among the weapons traded on the black market were hand grenades. Marshall Tito's soldiers were armed with the M75 grenade, manufactured in his own country. Inside its core are 3,000 steel balls capable of causing terrible and barely discriminate damage when detonated.

When Cregan tossed a 'pineapple' onto David Short's bullet-ridden body, he was using an M75 grenade from the former Yugoslavia.

It was the first time a grenade had been detonated in anger and used to harm someone in Britain during peacetime.

JUSTICE

In fact, by the time his murder trial got underway, there had only been four recorded hand grenade attacks in the UK, and Cregan was responsible for three of them.

The only other known grenade attack in the UK happened in Burton, Staffordshire, in March, 2011, when one was thrown at a terraced house as part of a feud between two gangs. No-one was hurt.

A month later, another hand grenade was discovered on a wall outside the Southport home of the former Liverpool footballer and manager Kenny Dalglish. Police found the device as part of a criminal investigation which had nothing to do with Dalglish.

Five men were later jailed over that incident and a series of shootings. The grenade wasn't detonated and so wasn't considered one of the four known attacks.

Cregan's exploits emphasised how serious criminals had access to, and were prepared to use, grenades.

During the time he was on the run, the police intelligence on Cregan suggested he had a 'bag full' of grenades – perhaps 20 or more – and that the going rate for one of them was anything up to £400. Police finally discovered Cregan's stash in a drain in Oldham shortly after his trial ended.

Police still do not know how many grenades are on the streets.

They tend to be manufactured in batches of 30,000 and so the working assumption is that there are plenty more still out there.

During the investigation, police brought in explosives expert Kevin Sanders, who examined what was left of Cregan's detonated grenades and the damage they caused.

GUNS AND GRENADES

Outside Sharon Hark's home in Luke Road, he found that a grenade had damaged a corner of the front of the property, destroying a concrete post and leaving 'shooting' marks on the wall at the front of the house.

The double-glazing had been damaged while a fragment from the grenade penetrated a UPVC door of a next-door neighbour's conservatory and smashed a window.

Among the blast damage at both crime scenes were a grenade safety pin, a metal spring from a firing mechanism, fly-off grenade levers and fuse assemblies. Unlike guns, grenades leave hardly anything which forensic experts can usefully examine for the purposes of a police investigation.

Grenades may have been Cregan's 'calling card', but he did far more damage with guns, particularly his weapon of choice – a Glock 9mm.

He admitted he had an arsenal of at least 10 guns, including semi-automatics like an Uzi and an AK47, although they were never found.

The bullets he used were from all over the world and even from a WWII Royal Ordnance factory. Criminals often find bullets harder to find than guns to fire them. Andre Botha, a ballistics expert, would later demonstrate inside a nervy courtroom just how powerful a specially adapted 9mm Glock could be.

That was the type of gun used to murder PCs Fiona Bone and Nicola Hughes in Mottram.

Handling the weapon in the witness stand in a hushed court, Mr Botha assured those gathered it had been de-commissioned and presented no risk to anyone.

"It's non-working. It's inert. There's no way anything can go wrong," said Mr Botha in the confident South African tones which had addressed many a trial where his considerable expertise on guns had been required.

The assurance wasn't entirely believed. It prompted nervous laughter in court before the judge, Mr Justice Holroyde, broke the tension by dead-panning: "Very encouraging news."

It was the cue for a little more laughter in court. But the half-hearted mirth couldn't disguise the very real tension. After all, it was a real Glock. But it was a demonstration model which could not be fired.

What followed was a workshop on how to fire the Austrian manufactured weapon and its safety mechanisms. Mr Botha pointed the gun in the air with his right hand as he showed how to cock the weapon. When it clicked, he said 'that's usually a sound you don't want to hear', to more nervous laughter.

Asked whether the weapon could be fired accidentally, he said: "With all the safety mechanisms built into this, if they are all functioning, this weapon can be dropped, jarred and bumped and it will not fire unless sufficient pressure is placed on the trigger."

Test firing of the Glock revealed Cregan must have used between 5.5 and 6lbs of pressure to pull the trigger. Mr Botha showed the court how preposterous it was to suggest the Glock could have gone off by accident.

Mr Botha continued to demonstrate how used cartridges were expelled from the barrel, occasionally aiming the gun into the pit of the court where the barristers were seated.

GUNS AND GRENADES

They would have been forgiven for ducking even though the weapon was a dud but they never flinched.

Later, the jurors – or at least those who wanted to – were handed a real and fully functioning Glock, the one Cregan used to murder the two police officers and David Short. They were invited to get a feel for the gun, and how hard it would have been to go off with minimal pressure on the trigger. Mr Botha took them through the rudiments of the weapon.

He told the court he had test fired the weapon and found it to be working normally. "It was fine. It would only discharge shots if it was cocked and pressure was applied to the trigger," he said.

After the Glock masterclass, he explained in detail what he believed had happened at Short home in Clayton.

The steep angle of a shot to Short's abdomen indicated he had been blasted while he was on or very close to the ground; of the five bullets found in his body, three were 9mm bullets and two .45 calibre bullets, indicating two weapons. At least 10 shots were fired at the scene, six of which were fired with the .45 calibre firearm. One shot was fired from the front door into the living room and had struck the wall adjoining the kitchen, the second shot was fired just inside the kitchen towards the cooker, the third shot was fired from inside the conservatory towards the patio doors, blasting through the window and then perforating the canvass of a chair out in the garden before bouncing off a glass table and smashing through the wooden door of the outhouse at the end of the garden and three further shots were fired in the walkway on the west side of the house.

Of the six bullets fired from the .45 calibre weapon, two were found in the house, one in the outhouse and one in the walkway while the remaining two were lodged in Short's body.

Of the four bullets fired from the 9mm Glock, three were found in Short's body and another was found near the outbuilding at the end of the back garden.

Police ballistics expert Helen Heavyside analysed the cartridges and bullet heads recovered from the crime scenes in Clayton, Droylsden and Mottram, and found they were from a variety of manufacturers, including dating back to World War II.

Some of the spent 9mm cartridges were made by IMI, an Israeli military manufacturer; CBC, a Brazilian manufacturer; MMS, a Czech manufacturer; and Winchester, an American brand. Amazingly, one of the casings found in the assassins' van had been produced in 1942 for the British military by a Royal Ordinance factory.

The Czech manufacturer, MMS, roughly translated as the Moravia Munitions Factory, came into existence in 1993 and filed for bankruptcy in 2003.

The supply of guns has long been a serious concern, particularly for GMP which has worked hard to tackle Manchester's notorious gangs based in the south of the city.

Around the turn of the century, machine guns had arrived and were causing havoc.

By 2005, police had taken most out of circulation, but found arms dealers had begun smuggling replica firearms into the country, mostly from eastern Europe and Germany.

A year later, almost half the weapons seized by GMP were

imitation weapons, made by companies like Cuno Melcher and Baikal, that had been adapted and converted to fire live rounds. Gunfighting in Greater Manchester reached its peak in 2007/8 with some 146 recorded shootings. Some 50 people were injured and six killed.

Innovative policing by XCalibre Taskforce – GMP's anti-gun and gang division in south Manchester – saw drastic reductions in the number of shootings.

It also helped that two of the city's most dangerous gangsters – Colin Joyce and Lee Amos – were jailed along with other gang members. In the 12-month period in which Cregan was committing his most serious crimes, there were only 34 shooting incidents, but they resulted in six deaths, four of them at Cregan's hands.

Despite the inroads in disrupting the supply of guns to Manchester's gangland, Dale Cregan showed that – away from the notorious Gooch and Doddington outfits of Moss Side – serious criminals elsewhere could still get their hands on serious weapons.

And not just starting pistols adapted to fire bullets but semi-automatics like Cregan's favourite, the Glock.

The guns may have been fired less often, but they could still cause loss of life.

They were still capable of destroying entire families and causing great sorrow.

16.

THE
TRIAL

February 4, 2013

The case against Cregan began at Preston Crown Court in the depths of winter.

However, it should not be forgotten that Cregan was not in the dock alone.

In fact, the dock was a very crowded place.

All in all, 10 people stood accused of various different crimes across the three incidents; the Cotton Tree killing of Mark Short, the gun and grenade attack on his father David and then the brutal slaying of PCs Hughes and Bone.

Cregan, Leon Atkinson, Luke Livesey, Damian Gorman, Ryan Hadfield and Matthew James were all accused of the murder of Mark Short and the attempted murders of three others also in the Cotton Tree at the time – John Collins, Ryan Pridding and Michael Belcher.

Cregan, Anthony Wilkinson, Francis Dixon and Jermaine Ward stood accused of the murder of David Short and all four were also jointly accused of the attempted murder of Sharon Hark on the same day, and a single charge of causing an explosion with a grenade.

Wilkinson faced a further charge of possession of a firearm with intent to endanger life while Irish Immie – real name Mohammed Imran Ali – was accused of assisting an offender.

No wonder the resulting case would take 77 days and cost £5m.

Journalists from all over the world wanted to cover the case and catch a glimpse of Cregan in the dock but such was the security that even getting into Court One was difficult.

Courts are supposed to be public places but, with a multiple murderer in the dock, the usual principle that justice should be seen to be done was severely limited. Journalists had to apply for tickets.

Up for grabs were just five press seats in the court itself and another 50 in a press annexe on the first floor, into which live pictures and sound from the court proper were beamed. Officially, the annexe was still a court of law. So journalists and court staff dutifully stood when the judge entered and left Court One downstairs. The ground-floor court itself was rather gloomy, particularly in the public gallery and press seats.

During the first few weeks of the case, the courtroom was packed. The families of PCs Bone and Hughes, and of David

THE TRIAL

Short, watched the proceedings from the public gallery, occasionally comforting each other when gruesome details of the murders were read out.

Of course, the whole experience was an ordeal for them.

They had to brave the massed ranks of photographers and camera crews outside. As is common practice in high-profile cases, they agreed to perform one walk into court so the cameramen could get their images, on the understanding they were left alone for the remainder of the trial.

Once inside court, they heard terrible details of how loved ones met their deaths. Beside them on the rather meagre fold-down seats in the public gallery were senior police officers who had investigated the case, and family liaison officers, tasked with providing the grieving families with pastoral support.

Journalists from the Manchester Evening News, the BBC, ITV, the Press Association and Sky were lucky enough to have tickets for the five press seats in the court, although only the MEN was there for every single day of the trial.

How much of an advantage the reporters in court – squeezed in at the very back of the room – had over the other journalists in the annexe, was debatable.

Between the press seats and the barristers were four rows of people, a smoked glass security screen and the witness stand, which was also boxed off with toughened glass.

In fact, it was almost impossible to see the QCs when they spoke, although the judge – sitting on his elevated platform – was just about within sight. It was even more difficult to see the dock at the rear of the building. Because of the angle, journalists had to peer through three of the smoked glass security screens and then through a fourth security screen of the dock itself before they could see the defendants. Cregan was on the far left of the dock, frequently sitting behind a computer monitor.

It meant a lot of craning of necks as reporters – and many others in the public gallery – tried to keep an eye on what the defendants were doing and saying. When the key players decided to give their own evidence, they stepped into the witness box.

All reporters in court could see was the back of a head.

And when the defendants themselves gave evidence, two of the five press seats were annexed by police officers in case the witness made a dash for it. Security was obviously important but it made rather a mockery of the principle of open justice.

In an era when the phone hacking scandal brought about by a small but significant group of rogue reporters shamed all of journalism, the arrangements for the media at Preston Crown Court left reporters in no doubt about where coverage of the case was on the judiciary's list of priorities.

Upstairs in the annexe, it was much brighter but not much better.

One camera beamed a picture of the judge and the witness stand to his left. Another showed the rows of barristers and solicitors, although some seated at the end of each row were out of shot.

A third camera showed a live picture of the dock, although Cregan and the others were only tiny, grainy figures in the distance. When the court occasionally went into secret session

– usually when a judge is asked in chambers to ensure a piece of evidence considered highly sensitive is kept out of the public part of the proceedings – the live feed was switched off.

On at least one occasion, staff in the court forgot to inform colleagues in the annexe that the court was back in public session. It wasn't for long but showed the practical difficulties in such a high-profile case.

As the days dragged on, interest from many media in the case waned as the prosecution focused on the murder of Mark Short in the Cotton Tree.

The national newspapers, BBC and Sky were mainly interested in the murder of the two police officers and it would be many weeks before the prosecution got to that.

However, they probably wished they had lingered a little longer on day four. There had been a rumour earlier in the day that it might be worth 'sticking around'.

The rumours were right. Sensationally right in fact.

As other news outlets slipped away, the MEN stayed and scooped its rivals with the bombshell that Dale Cregan had dramatically changed his plea and admitted the murder of PCs Fiona Bone and Nicola Hughes, although he still maintained he was innocent of the other charges he faced.

Finally, Cregan accepted responsibility.

He knew there was no possible way he would be acquitted.

The trail leading back to him was red hot and the amount of evidence produced by GMP was simply too much to fight against.

The news that Cregan had pleaded guilty to the murder of the police officers was broken on the paper's website through its rolling blog on the trial. Journalists all around Manchester turned on their heels and hurried back to Preston.

One of them was about to get in the bath when he got a frantic call from his newsdesk.

The news was soon everywhere and prompted seven pages in the MEN the following day, quite a feat considering they were inspired by Cregan saying just one word: 'guilty'.

Of course, it was a dramatic development but the truth was the change of heart came about in rather matter-of-fact circumstances.

In the absence of the jury before the afternoon session began, the judge was told Cregan now wanted to plead guilty to the murder of the two officers.

The jurors were brought in and his QC, the relatively helpless Mr Simon Csoka, simply invited the clerk of the court to put those charges again to his client.

He stood and after each of the two counts was read to him, he simply said: "guilty".

He sat down and the trial continued.

There was no fanfare inside court, although plenty outside as news spread about Cregan's about-face.

Why exactly he changed his mind remained something of a mystery. Up until that point, he was considering pleading insanity.

Perhaps his mother, Anita, had something to do with it.

The rumour was that she had visited him that weekend at Strangeways. The reason may have been simpler.

By then, the series of revealing interviews he had conducted with the psychologist and psychiatrist in prison had been completed. Perhaps he just didn't want the more personal details he had revealed to come out, as they would have done had he continued with such a defence.

Prison is an unforgiving environment at the best of times. It cannot be any better if the world knows your sexual foibles or that you are a bed-wetter.

For a macho man like Cregan, reputation was all important.

Although Cregan had changed his plea on the murders of the two police officers, he remained adamant that he had not murdered Mark Short and then his father, David.

He also insisted he was not guilty of the attempted murder of Sharon Hark after throwing a grenade at her house shortly after shooting dead David Short.

That ensured that the case would continue and he would still be tried for those crimes.

Cregan's QC, Mr Csoka, was commended by the judge for his skill in defending his client but the truth was his hands were tied by Cregan.

He had been gagged. Cregan could have run a 'diminished responsibilities' defence with a sporting chance of success.

For an unknown reason, he opted against that.

Literally, Cregan and his barrister offered no defence. It was baffling and a little embarrassing for Mr Csoka, who could do nothing.

The QC tried to keep the damning confession Cregan had given to the psychologist and psychiatrist in prison from the jury, but to no avail.

After catching the waiting media on the hop by admitting

to the murders of PCs Bone and Hughes, Cregan then pulled another surprise just before the end of the trial.

The jurors must have been wondering what on earth Mr Csoka could say on his client's behalf as the closing speeches began.

Cregan had told everyone bar the court he was guilty – the psychiatrist and psychologist, his mum, his co-defendants and he had also tried to bully and coerce them into protecting him as the trial dragged on and on.

The fact he had murdered David Short was the 'worst kept secret in Strangeways', according to the Crown's QC, Nicholas Clarke.

All the evidence had been heard across 16 weeks of the trial.

Now the defending barristers were making their closing speeches.

And Mr Csoka's was remarkable.

He simply invited the clerk of the court to put six of the seven remain counts to Cregan again.

Wearing his grey hoodie and jogging bottoms, Cregan stood as he had two months before and simply responded 'guilty' to those charges.

He formally admitted murdering Mark and David Short, attempting to murder three others in the Cotton Tree pub and throwing the grenade at Sharon Hark's home.

Controlling to the end, he wanted to be convicted by his own plea and not by the verdict of a jury.

He didn't want to give them – or the Shorts who were watching in the public gallery – the satisfaction of being found guilty.

However, he insisted he was still not guilty of the one remaining charge, that he had attempted to murder Sharon Hark.

Yes he had chucked the grenade but, no, he did not mean to kill anyone.

He was adamant about that and his defence, Mr Csoka, provided an interesting angle to underline that Cregan had never intended to kill Sharon Hark.

He told the jurors: "Those guilty pleas are probably of little surprise to you. You have probably wondered 'what is going on?', 'what are those two barristers (Csoka and his junior) doing', 'they don't seem to be asking many questions or challenging anyone?'.

"We are dealing with someone who, when he sets out to kill, he kills.

"When he set out to kill Mark Short, he killed him. When he set out to kill David Short, he killed him. When he set out to kill the police officers, he did. There was never any danger of him failing to carry out those murderous objectives."

The message was clear. If Cregan had wanted to murder Sharon Hark, he would have done so.

Cregan's admissions were a further dramatic chapter in a trial that contained many twists.

The public didn't know it at the time, but the trial came close to collapse as early as day six.

Mr Clarke had delivered his opening address for the Crown and was on his third day of presenting evidence when the expensive juggernaut came to a juddering halt thanks to an outspoken juror who told his colleagues: "They are all guilty as fuck and we don't have to listen all day to this shite."

It was leapt on by defence barristers who suggested the whole jury should be discharged and a new one sworn in.

The offending juror had been grassed up by a colleague and he was turfed off the panel without – strange as it seems – even the chance of a fair hearing.

Mr Justice Holroyde decided in the end that the juror's actions had not been grave enough to cancel the entire trial. The offending juror was released and the trial continued with an 11-person jury instead of the usual 12.

The judge had many problems to contend with, including an argument with the barristers involved in the case as they wished to go out on strike in protest at Government plans to slash £220m from the legal aid bill.

The barristers argued earnestly outside court that it wasn't about fat-cat lawyers being allowed to continue to feather their own nests. It was about the future of the judicial system. Their argument was not helped when one of them let it be known times were so tough he'd been forced to do his own garden that week! And when one suggested a picket line with patio heaters, a colleague had to tell him a burning oil drum was the custom.

The judge made it plain he would not countenance a delay in the proceedings.

With his dire warning still ringing in their ears, the lawyers later backed down. Mr Clarke, again speaking for all the barristers, said they would bow to the judge's wishes after 'careful and anxious consideration'.

THE TRIAL

These issues, alongside the gargantuan cost of the trial, occasional prejudicial Twitter posts and even controversial comments made by Home Secretary Theresa May, all added up.

May announced halfway through trial that she wanted police killers locked up for life. It was hardly a surprising statement from the Government minister but it did shine the spotlight even stronger on Preston Crown Court at a time when Mr Justice Holroyde was keen for the jury not to be swayed by strong announcements from public figures.

All in all, it was a testing trial for everyone, for many reasons.

17.

HONOUR AMONG THIEVES

The jurors may have been stretched to their limits as early as day six, but they had their hands full throughout the trial as they did their best to separate truth from fiction.

The lying and deceit witnessed was on an industrial scale and although those in the dock may have been accused of being partners in crime, they soon turned on each other when in the witness box.

A particular tactic was to blame the 'lunatic' Cregan, claiming he had acted on his own.

Cregan had, of course, pleaded guilty early on to the deaths of PCs Bone and Hughes but remained staunchly adamant about the other crimes he had been involved with.

His fellow co-defendants were desperate not to go down with him and the first to blame Cregan solely for the summer of bloodshed was his old friend and gym partner Leon 'Acky' Atkinson.

JUSTICE

LEON ATKINSON

Leon had been pals with Cregan for eight years. He liked to portray himself as a hard-working family man, a father of two daughters living in Squires Lane in Tyldesley.

With his business partner Billy Black, the pair renovated houses in Manchester. He also worked as a gas fitter.

He and Cregan would do weights together at Ultimate Fitness. Of course, the pair loved the boxing training room. They would enjoy the sauna there and, afterwards, go to Nando's for a bite to eat.

"He was a good friend," Leon told the jurors in his trial, who could not have failed to spot the use of the past tense.

Atkinson tried hard to distance himself from one of his best mates, the 'lunatic' who had admitted murdering two police officers.

It wouldn't suit his defence to be seen to be close to a self-confessed killer. Whether the acrimony he suggested was real or not was unclear, but he certainly put as much daylight as he could between himself and Cregan.

Atkinson had to explain the flurry of calls between him, his mother, Theresa, and Cregan after she had been slapped in the Cotton Tree 12 days before the killing of Mark Short.

Atkinson told the jury that he had been with his brother Frankie to watch City win the Premier League at The Etihad Stadium and then went to The Manchester pub to celebrate.

He described how 'football hooligans' started causing trouble, among them a mate of Cregan – Steven Garvey – the same man Cregan would summon the night before he murdered two police officers.

Leon got involved in a brawl with the 'hooligans' and suffered a cut lip and a rip to his jacket. The man he brawled with threatened to come to his house but Leon was keen to avoid this and wanted to arrange a 'meet'. Leon then called Cregan so he could then ring Garvey to get in touch with the man with whom he had fought.

Whether the post-game brawl he described in The Manchester ever happened is unclear, but Atkinson made no secret of the fact he liked to settle arguments with his fists and he was certainly the type of man who would get into scrapes just like the one he described.

"That's how I would sort something out if I had a problem: with my fists," he said. No-one doubted him.

He said he was at a mate's flat when his 'drunk' mother Theresa called him on his mobile, telling him all about how she had just been slapped.

"I knew it would have been her because she's trouble when she's drunk. She didn't know what had happened. I knew it would have been down to her mouthing off. She was bladdered. I know what my mum's like when she's had a beer," he told the court.

Leon sought to explain why he felt the need to speak to the Shorts on the phone a couple of days later.

He claimed he wanted to contact Raymond Young to find out what had gone on.

He told the jury that he had been convinced by the explanation from Young, that he had 'clipped' his mother as she went at him repeatedly with a bottle. Young, he suggested, had been apologetic while David Short brushed off the spat with laughter and suggested flowers and chocolates should be sent round to Theresa to say sorry and draw a line under the row.

Atkinson declined the offer as 'not necessary'.

"I was embarrassed at how my mum had been behaving. I was just embarrassed. I knew she had not been slapped for nothing so I was happy. I told her she had been carrying on and she had bottled him. I had a go at her, for drinking in scruffy pubs and carrying on like that," he said, before going on to point the finger of blame at his mate Cregan.

"There was no scheme put together. If Cregan's done something, he's done it off his own back on the spur of the moment," Atkinson said.

"There's never been any such plan. I don't go around shooting people. That's not the way I am.... I'm here because of other people's actions. Somebody has gone mad with a gun and killed someone and I'm here because of that. I'm here because of other people's actions. It was a spur of the moment thing. He was drinking all day. There's been no plan. He has been out drinking all day and he's done what he's done."

He may have kept his receipts from his trip to Wales but Atkinson also had to explain his sudden departure from the caravan park in Prestatyn back to Manchester once Mark Short had been killed.

To that end he told the jury about a mysterious figure he had eye-balled at the campsite.

He suggested that perhaps the Shorts had sent someone to

follow his mother to the caravan park. "When she arrived, not long afterwards there was a man who came past the caravan looking in and looking suspicious. I thought she had been followed by one of the Shorts. I don't really know what I thought. It just freaked me out, so I just left," Atkinson told his trial.

He claimed he didn't return to his home in Tyldesley because of fears of reprisals. Reprisal for what? He tried to suggest he and his family were in mortal danger because of a false rumour.

"David Short is known as a hard man. With his son dying in his arms, I was worried for my family," said Atkinson.

Atkinson continued to abandon any notion of friendship with Cregan as the defence continued with him suggesting that he 'started hearing rumours within a week that Dale might have been responsible'.

He continued: "You have seen Dale Cregan. He's a lunatic. You have seen what he's done with the police women. He has been out drinking all day.

"He's found out they were in the Cotton Tree and done what he's done."

LUKE LIVESEY

The next person to step onto the witness stand was another Ultimate Fitness regular, Luke Livesey, the 'muscle' Cregan had recruited for the Cotton Tree hit.

And Livesey might have got away with murder had he not got so tangled in the yarn he span.

The pair became firm friends after Cregan sold Livesey a truck in around 2006. Livesey, also a regular eBay trader, would swing by Cregan's house in Hyde or his mother Anita's house in Droylsden, when he lived there, before driving the pair of them to the gym for a workout.

They would go almost every day during the week. The pair, along with Ryan Hadfield and Matty James, formed a close group of friends.

On the day of the Mark Short murder, Livesey and Cregan had made their regular visit to the gym during the morning before they met up again at Livesey's girlfriend's house in Mottram, where their getaway driver, Damian Gorman, was busy laying concrete foundations for a new shed.

Ryan Hadfield, Cregan's best pal, turned up and, after the work was complete, they all went to a local boozer, The Waggon. It was the start of what it suited Livesey to describe as an all-day bender which took in seven pubs, and lots of alcohol.

Next was the Hare and Hounds in nearby Werneth Low towards Stockport before the party headed north to the Wetherspoon's pub in Stalybridge, where the drinking continued apace.

Later they popped next door for a drink in the Lord Stamford. Pints of lager and bottles of Kopparberg cider were downed, punctuated by Jaeger bombs. By the time they moved onto The Organ, also in Stalybridge, everyone was 'very, very drunk', according to Livesey. And the designated driver that night, despite getting hammered, was Livesey.

He told the jury he drove Cregan to another pub, the Prince of Wales, and waited in the car park, but he never came out. Livesey's story was that he drove back to his girlfriend's house in Mottram, rowed with her, tried to have sex and when his advances were rejected, he fell asleep while Cregan was committing murder at the Cotton Tree.

It was a lie.

Livesey contorted himself into knots trying to explain away telephone evidence, which showed the movements and communication before and after the killing.

It meant Livesey had to explain why he still had a phone he claimed he had left with Cregan.

The barely credible answer was that Cregan, having committed the murder, posted the phone through the letterbox at the house in Mottram.

Another lie.

While he was on remand at Strangeways on the same wing as Cregan, Livesey continued with the lying and penned himself an alibi for Cregan to sign. Effectively, it wrote Livesey out of the murder.

But it was only to be used as a last resort by Cregan, whose case was correctly regarded as hopeless. It entailed Cregan confessing to the Mark Short murder as well as putting his mate in the clear.

In the confession, Cregan would say he had left Livesey because he was drunk and had been arguing with his girlfriend.

Livesey, according to the script, had made his way alone towards Glossop while Cregan and another unnamed man went to pick up the gun before heading to the Cotton Tree for the murder.

Another big fat lie.

"Only use if I'm desperate," wrote Livesey. Cregan never

signed on the dotted line as Livesey had suggested, perhaps hoping against hope he could still somehow escape justice.

At the time it was discovered, Cregan was still denying all four of the murder charges he faced.

When it was uncovered in a search of Cregan's cell, it was a hammer blow to Livesey's efforts to evade justice. It wasn't the only incriminating document to be uncovered.

The prison authorities also found a second 'confession', this time in Livesey's cell in which Anthony Wilkinson – not even charged with the Mark Short murder – admitted it was him and not Livesey in the stolen car which took the assassins to the Cotton Tree.

Another lie.

He also claimed a third confession cleared his name, this time apparently from the unnamed man who had gone to the Cotton Tree with Cregan. First Livesey told the jurors Cregan hadn't told him the man's name and within minutes changed his mind but refused to reveal it to the court. He was warned by the judge that the jurors would be entitled to 'draw inferences' from his refusal to answer a legitimate question.

Livesey stuck to his guns and piously said: "I wasn't willing to bring a rumour into court." Of course, he didn't want to name anyone because it could have been exposed as a fiction and his already paper-thin defence would have disintegrated still further.

His efforts to pull the wool over the eyes of the jurors were determined and numerous, but they weren't terribly sophisticated.

HONOUR AMONG THIEVES

As part of its case, the prosecution played a compilation of CCTV footage showing the three Mark Short assassins walking single file through Hollingworth and heading to the house where they would get cleaned up after committing the murder and after torching the getaway car.

The three figures – Cregan, Livesey and Damien Gorman – were all around the same height. Livesey took his shoes off before he stepped onto the witness stand to make himself appear shorter.

It was spotted by prosecutor Mr Clarke and a sheepish Livesey claimed it was because he had sore feet. Livesey, at 5ft 10in tall, tried to suggest he was around 5ft 8in.

Another problem with his story was that Anthony Wilkinson – the man Livesey would have the jury believe had taken part in the murder instead of him – was 6 foot-plus.

In fact, it appeared Livesey had struck a deal with Cregan, who would try to take sole responsibility for the Mark Short murder in return for a promise that Livesey would look after Cregan's family while he was in prison.

Livesey feigned exasperation at the suggestion: "This is rubbish, complete rubbish. I have told you about a confession from two people. I have also obtained a confession from a third individual. I just don't know what more you want me to do... I'm an innocent man and I shouldn't be here today."

The case against Livesey was centred mostly on the telephone evidence.

There was no forensic evidence linking him to the crime.

As his QC Paul Reid pointed out, the Crown's case against

his client was entirely circumstantial. Without his cack-handed attempts to create 'confessions' to put him in the clear, the jury may have found it a little more difficult to convict him.

DAMIAN GORMAN

Cregan's getaway driver for the Cotton Tree murder, Damian 'Scarface' Gorman, told yet more lies to the jury and, in fact, created a shambolic courtroom performance out of his deceit.

Career criminal Gorman had been given the name because a sizeable scar disfigured him, and it was a title he revelled in.

From dealing drugs, to counterfeit cash and nicking cars, Scarface had tried his hand at most crimes.

And a threatening demeanour to go along with his facial disfigurement was a handy tool he picked up along the way.

Gorman had been holidaying in Spain when he got the call from Cregan, but he was soon on the team.

He was regarded as an expert getaway driver and he had tried his hand at most forms of crime, but cars were his thing.

He was at the wheel in the stolen blue Ford Focus which had carried Cregan and Luke Livesey to and from the Cotton Tree.

And he played a crucial role in trying to cover the tracks after the murder. He guided the gang to the property in Hollingworth where they dumped clothes and got cleaned up after the assassination. The car was burned out nearby.

Gorman met Cregan for the first time in about 2005 through a cousin and they became friends, although in court he was keen to belittle Cregan, describing him as boisterous and moody, especially during nights out.

Whatever was said in court, Cregan could rely on Gorman to be his driver on the night because he knew the back roads well and would be able to drive the gang away from the scene unnoticed.

And he could also provide a bolt-hole where they assassins could clean up after the killing.

Gorman had previously rented the property, on Moorfield Terrace, and had only moved out four months earlier. He knew it was empty.

Cregan, Livesey and Gorman climbed in through a window and got cleaned up while their getaway car burned on the other side of the village. Among the items found by police later was a balaclava with Gorman's DNA.

Making something of a spectacle of himself in court, he tried to claim he had simply used the mask to keep warm while he was riding 'crosses', or motocross bikes, on the local fields. He insisted that when he had worn it while riding bikes he had not pulled it down to cover his entire face, forgetting that his DNA had been found around the mouth hole.

As he stood on the witness stand, he tried on the balaclava and tried to manipulate it to suggest how it could be worn innocently and also in a manner that could explain his DNA round the mouth hole.

In court he may have been a laughing stock.

Outside it, he certainly wasn't.

Ten days after the shooting, Gorman had got heavy with a

woman he feared was talking to the police. He made a cut-throat gesture and told her 'the one-eyed Scotchman' would be knocking on her door if she told the police anything, a clear reference to his pal Cregan.

He told her: "You better make sure that you keep your fucking mouth shut or you're dead." He went on in the same vein later: "What the fuck did you say to the police?... You see these people, what they are capable of. You're fucking next. You and your fucking kids." Gorman had made it plain he was a drug dealer in the most menacing way – within a few minutes of meeting the woman he had offered her a line of cocaine on the tip of a long knife. "I was really intimidated by the man. I was petrified of him. Many people are," she said.

Gorman had shown he had access to guns and was rather an expert when it came to terrorising people who got in his way. He had once pulled a gun on a pub landlord who had barred him. David Doughty, licensee at the Silver Springs pub in Denton, had barred Gorman and some of his friends in 2004. Eventually, he allowed some of Gorman's pals back into the boozer, but not Gorman himself, who was irked at being singled out. So he simply defied the ban and turned up one night. When Doughty saw him drinking outside the pub, he went to have words.

Gorman reacted with the menace that became a trademark, telling the landlord he was 'making me look like a cunt in front of my mates'. He pulled aside his jacket to reveal a gun in his trousers.

The landlord made a complaint to the police but later

withdrew it, claiming he did not want to pour fuel onto the flames.

When police spoke to Doughty and his partner again after the Cotton Tree murder about the incident in 2004, the pair were as reticent as they were at the time, and refused to attend court to explain to the jury just how menacing Gorman could be.

They were summonsed anyway and, under threat of arrest, reluctantly gave evidence in the murder trial. Doughty, giving evidence from behind screens where he could not see or be seen by Gorman, admitted as much in front of the jury, saying he 'didn't want to be mithered and just want to get on with my life'.

Gorman gave a remarkable performance while he was on the witness stand, with many of his answers little more than a series of scarcely formed ideas which were forced together in tortuous and barely intelligible sentences.

He certainly was jittery and constantly apologising for little outbursts. Often he embarked on speeches to answer questions which hadn't been asked, and had to be warned by the judge.

At one stage he called the prosecutor, Mr Clarke, a 'smart arse'. Mid-way through the trial he threatened to sack his QC, Ray Wigglesworth, who would have been forgiven for being disappointed when his client later changed his mind.

Gorman's favourite line, which he used on perhaps a dozen occasions during his evidence, was: "I'm here to tell the truth. I'm not here to lie."

The jury saw straight through him.

Gorman admitted he had been drinking with Cregan in the

hours before the Cotton Tree shooting but claimed – at the time the murder happened – he had returned to his home in Thomas Street, Glossop, to be with his heavily pregnant girlfriend of three years, Sarah Clarke, who was 15 years younger. She had been four-months pregnant at the time and went on to have Gorman's son on September 1, 2012, while he was in prison awaiting trial.

She appeared as one of his defence witnesses, saying that she had thrown out the incriminating items found outside the Moorfield Terrace property after he had been sent to prison for another offence. She had dumped them simply because they were dirty, she said. She denied suggestions she was willing to lie to make sure her baby had a father who wasn't in prison.

The jurors were told she had been charged with intimidating a prosecution witness, the woman who claimed Gorman had threatened her with the 'one-eyed Scotchman'. It was an offence she denied during her boyfriend's murder trial. "How could I intimidate her? I was four months pregnant. If I was going to threaten her, I would have done it a long time before. I never threatened her," she said.

RYAN HADFIELD

Cregan's best friend, Ryan Hadfield, was also accused of being involved in the Cotton Tree murder as the prosecution claimed he acted as one of Cregan's spotters in the pub, letting him know when the Short family had arrived and where in the pub they were located.

HONOUR AMONG THIEVES

Hadfield had known Cregan since the age of 10 when they were at school together.

When they grew up in Droylsden, they lived just a few streets away from each other. In adulthood, they spoke every day on the phone, went out drinking at weekends and went on lads holidays.

The father of a young daughter, Hadfield tried his best to create an image of a hard-working family man. He had worked briefly as a plasterer and pipe fitter. He had also worked for Central Electrical, a firm of electrical contractors based in Cheetham Hill, Manchester.

For a time, he worked as a plasterer for Darren Merriman, the father of Cregan's girlfriend, Georgia Merriman. But by the middle of 2010, he turned to crime full-time and abandoned any pretence that he was making an honest living.

He became a cannabis farmer, and business was lucrative. It meant he always had cash in his pocket and could afford to live a jet-set lifestyle. He enjoyed many foreign trips, some of them with his best friend.

Hadfield went carp fishing in France with Cregan and Cregan's brother, Dean. The pair went on a lads holiday to Amsterdam in December, 2011, just a few months before the murder to celebrate a 40th.

Hadfield tried to play down his life of crime and expensive foreign trips during the trial for obvious reasons.

The flights and hotel had been cheap for the Amsterdam trip, he said. But the price of the fights and hotel were not really matters he was worried about because he always had plenty of cash.

JUSTICE

In fact, when police stopped him once in a hire van in Ancoats, they found him with a box containing £49,000 in dirty cash, no doubt the proceeds of his drug dealing. He was also wearing a £2,000 Rolex, also bought with criminal money. He was later convicted of money laundering. He tried to play down the Rolex during his murder trial. "It wasn't that nice," he said, unconvincingly.

In court he acknowledged Cregan was a serious criminal while he was on the witness stand, and repeatedly said his friend 'would never ask' him to get involved in anything really heavy like a murder.

"I'm not the sort of person who would do something like that. I don't even know any of the Shorts," he said.

It wasn't just the defendants who gave nervy performances in court – some of the witnesses got in on the act too.

Taxi driver Kamran Nazir had given a lift to Cregan and some his accomplices just before the murder at the Cotton Tree. His evidence about the movements and identities of the murderers was important.

In court, he had a sudden attack of amnesia. Nazir had been categoric when he gave a statement to the police about the men he had picked up on the night of the murder: first he picked up a customer 'Luke' and two others from The Organ pub in Stalybridge and then went on to pick up a fourth man from the New Inn pub in nearby Hollingworth, a regular with a scar on his face he knew as 'Damo'.

When he stood in the witness box at Preston Crown Court, suddenly he told a very different story.

In his frequently rambling and inconsistent testimony, he repeatedly insisted he had not known any of the customers who had stepped into his cab that night, and nor was he sure even how many men had got into his taxi. Perhaps it should not have been a surprise.

The jury was unaware the police had struggled to get hold of him to confirm he was to give evidence in the trial. He only confirmed his attendance on the day he was scheduled to appear on the witness stand. Mr Nazir had also belatedly asked to give evidence from behind screens, so no-one in the dock or public gallery could see him.

The prosecutor, Mr Clarke, tried manfully to keep any sense of frustration from the jury when the man in front of him was clearly not sticking to the script, namely the police statements he had been happy to sign a few months before. Had he seen any of these customers before?

Did any of them have any distinctive facial features? The questions were supposed to elicit the response he had given in his statements, that a regular customer called Damo with a scar on his face had got into the cab, and even that he could recall he had been sitting in the middle of the three men in the rear of his taxi. Perhaps he had been nobbled.

That was certainly the suspicion of the police officers watching from the public gallery.

At the end of his tether, the Mr Clarke requested for the jury to be taken out of court and asked the judge to allow Mr Nazir to be treated as a hostile witness. Mr Justice Holroyde agreed, but only at the second time of asking.

He finally agreed to allow the prosecutor off his leash after the witness continued to stonewall. "It did seem to me there was a most marked contrast between the detailed statement and professed complete inability to remember anything what-so-ever about these passengers or remember any distinguishing features of any passengers," said the judge.

He had found Mr Nazir to be 'evasive', somehow managing to remember very many inconsequential details of the journey but yet unable to recall anything significant to the prosecution's case.

The following day, Mr Nazir squirmed uncomfortably in the witness box as the police statements he had signed were read out to him by Mr Clarke.

In them, he told the police the details of the fare were so unusual they 'stick in my mind'. The statement said he picked up three men at The Organ pub and that he believed initially he was to take the men to Droylsden.

During the journey, one of the customers seemed to be having an argument with a woman on a mobile phone. When the taxi got to Acres Lane area of Stalybridge, one of the passengers asked him to divert to Hollingworth, where two men got out at the New Inn.

One of these two went into the pub and another went around the side. It wasn't part of his police statement, and nor could he have known it, but perhaps the assassins had just picked up the gun which was to be used in the murder.

A few minutes later, the men returned with a fourth man Mr Nazir said he knew as a regular customer called Damo with a scar on his face who used to regularly take taxis between the New Inn and The Organ. The witness could not have been clearer.

Asked in court whether the first statement he had signed was true, Mr Nazir gave a rambling, unconvincing reply: "Yes and no. I can't honestly say Damo or the chap by the name Damo, whether he got out. Obviously on certain jobs you do certain things you remember and certain things you don't remember. I know that a couple of them got out at Stalybridge. Initially, I didn't remember that.

"Afterwards I recalled the fact. I remember me braking at the lights. It's not something I'm used to. The sheer volume of jobs, your judgement is affected. You think you remember certain jobs but you are remembering another job... You are constantly on the same roads and on the same routes. You are always on the road and very tired."

Not for the first time, it looked very much like Gorman had somehow managed to put the frighteners on a police witness.

Mr Clarke was like a dog with a bone. He put it to the discomfited Mr Nazir that his memory was not so bad that he could not remember in his police statement that one of the customers in the back was very athletic.

The tension was broken – but not the lingering suspicion the witness had been nobbled – when his ludicrously detailed response prompted some laughter in court: "He had good legs. he had very defined legs and he had a tan. I'm not being funny, but if you see somebody with good legs – they've got good legs."

The man he was describing was Cregan.

Perhaps shocked at the incredulity that was evident in court, he prompted yet more laughter when he said: "It's not that he had an extra leg or anything."

"I don't agree with you," he then told Mr Clarke, who had suggested he had been lying to the jury and being evasive.

The disparity between Mr Nazir's statements and courtroom comments was actually not too significant in the grand scheme of the Crown's case.

The prosecution was able to establish beyond doubt Gorman was among the assassins and he would be convicted.

What everyone was waiting for was Cregan to give evidence. He never did.

But his mother, Anita, did.

She chose the 44th day of her son's murder trial to finally speak up. She had not done so during her son's defence for the simple reason he had not offered, nor called, a single witness.

Instead, she appeared in court as a witness for one of his co-accused and friend, Francis Dixon.

FRANCIS DIXON

Dixon was up in court on the same charges as Cregan and Anthony Wilkinson over the killing of David Short.

He may not have been present at the time, but the prosecution claimed that he aided and abetted to such an extent that he deserved to be consider a co-accused.

Dixon denied he had been one of the orchestrators of David Short's death and professed to being shocked when Cregan rang him to admit his part in the crime.

He never denied picking up Anita after Cregan had asked him to keep his mum safe following Short's death.

He admitted he had spoken to Cregan after the crime but he insisted his involvement ended there and that he was just trying to protect Anita from any potential revenge attack.

"All I have done is be stupid to try to help somebody, a life-long friend, point them in the right direction. That's it," he told the jury. And they believed him.

While her son was on the run, Anita made no public utterances, although she contacted the Manchester Evening News to complain about what she thought were the gratuitous references to her son as a 'one-eyed fugitive'.

The mother of four grown-up children gave her evidence from behind screens, apparently afraid of those who might be watching from the public gallery, among them members of the Short clan.

Screens or not, her performance was far from timid during two days of remarkable evidence.

And her message was loud and clear.

Her Dale wasn't to blame. For blame, she looked elsewhere: at the police who had 'hounded' her and who created 'turmoil' in her life. She also blamed Matty James who she claimed had manipulated her son into causing a bloodbath.

MATTY JAMES

James was dragged into the investigation into the Cotton Tree murders because of his friendship with Cregan and the fact he was drinking in the pub the night Cregan leapt into action.

About an hour before he shot dead Mark Short, Dale Cregan called James, a petty criminal he had known since they were both teenagers.

Cregan knew his old mate was a regular in the Cotton Tree and he wanted to be sure Raymond Young was there.

"Have you seen him with your own eyes?" asked Cregan.

James, a bricklayer, had indeed seen Young walk into the pub with his own eyes, along with David Short and John Short, aka John Collins.

In fact, he had shaken hands with John Short to 'keep him sweet' when he arrived. The Shorts all knew James was a friend of the hated Cregan and so he had to be careful.

James had been in his favourite pub – he knew the landlord – with his dad and others since 2pm, watching the racing and placing bets in the bookies just down the road. When he saw the Short clan walking into the boozer, he knew he had to make himself scarce.

He left the pub about 9.45pm and headed home to Clayton in a taxi. It was on the journey home he got his first call from Cregan asking if Raymond Young was in the pub.

"Yeah. Why?" said James, and Cregan replied: "Never you mind why."

James said: "Don't you be fucking causing trouble in there because they've just seen me leave there."

"Fuck them lot," said Cregan, who most certainly would be causing trouble.

HONOUR AMONG THIEVES

Knowing Raymond Young and other members of the Short clan were in the Cotton Tree, he could begin to prepare for the murder, having used his old friend to make sure the targets were exactly where he wanted them.

After eventually hearing that Cregan had dished out his own form of justice, James fully understood that he was likely to be implicated, but he was not willing to go down for Cregan, Livesey and Gorman's actions.

He was arrested on suspicion of the murder of Mark Short and although he said nothing to the police, he changed his attitude during the trial and told the jury that he had been an unwitting player in a violent game.

James also knew that his life was at risk for refusing to remain silent.

"I've come here to tell the truth," he told all the defence barristers arranged in front of him in court. "I know you lot are all going to have a go at me. I know you are much more intelligent than me. That night changed my life forever, but I'm not giving in.

"My intention was not to grass.

"I have chosen not to listen to any of them and stand up here and tell the truth. I've gone past caring."

James flashed an angry look over at the dock when he was asked whether he was trying to save his own skin.

He said: "I'm the man standing here – I'm not a coward... You're damn right I'm trying to save my own skin. I've done nothing wrong. I didn't know what was going to happen that night. It was my local pub. I wouldn't have sent someone in there to do a shooting in there with all my mates still there."

Cregan raised his eyebrows in the dock when James spoke about how he had shown 'loyalty' but didn't want to 'give my life up for something I didn't do'. "It's not just 10 years. It's the rest of my life. They shouldn't be expecting that of someone like me. I'm just a normal working guy. I was trying to make a lie to help other people when I just didn't know what was going on. It's too much to expect," he said.

He said he felt ill after learning David Short had been murdered three months later: "The reason why I didn't want to pass information on is because people know where my family are. When you find out somebody has been shot and bombed, it's not so something you want to be speaking about, so I kept my mouth shut."

His family had panic alarms fitted and James realised his revelations made him a marked man for the rest of his life: "I'll be killed. I will probably be killed after this case because I'm telling the truth. I have got information of what people are telling me to say. I will probably be killed some time after this."

James' willingness to implicate Cregan and his accomplices caused much friction during the case.

And Anita Cregan was particularly upset that James had spoken.

As far as she was concerned, even if her son had had pulled the trigger, others were to blame for the killing spree.

If she was to be believed, her love for her son was literally unquestioning.

Even though he privately confessed to all four murders to her when he was locked up, she claimed never to have asked him why he had embarked on a murder spree or where he had hidden the grenades or who else had helped him.

Quizzing her son would have been 'unfair'.

She finished with an apology but there was no grand effort to reach out to the grieving families of the two police officers her son had slaughtered.

The remorse she expressed on her son's behalf was for the pain he had caused the Cregan family, not his victims. "He's sorry, sorry for wrecking our lives," she said.

Her appearance had been shrouded in secrecy. Two days before she got onto the witness stand, the jurors had only been told of the impending and mysterious appearance of someone who 'cannot be named'.

Finally, she swore on the bible to tell the whole truth and gave her evidence from behind screens.

Even though her identity was no secret and her appearance known to many, she was treated as a protected witness.

Those in the dock, including her son, couldn't see her.

Only the judge, jury and some of the lawyers in court could actually watch her as she gave evidence. The judge would later add another layer of protection, prohibiting the media from publishing any pictures of her, her place of work or her address.

Like others, she was on the police 'threat to life' register, so the risk was obvious, but quite how a picture and an address of someone who had been personally visited by a member of the Short family to issue a threat increased the risk she already faced, was difficult to fathom.

The order was lifted after a challenge from the Press.

Dixon had called Anita as a witness because he wanted her to confirm what had passed between them when he had driven her to a safehouse after the murder of David Short.

And as well as acting as a witness for Dixon, Anita also tried to explain to the court why it was all the fault of Matty James.

On the evening of the Cotton Tree murders, Anita said she had thrown James and her older son, Dean Cregan, out of her house as they had become too loud and drunk.

They had been partying during a warm night on the decking at the rear of her bungalow.

Instead, they moved onto Anita's eldest daughter Kelly's house nearby to carry on the drinking.

At about 6am the following morning, Kelly called her mum to report Dean was giving Matty 'a good hiding'.

Anita went round and Dean told her 'mum, he's a piece of shit'.

Angry Dean Cregan was booting James as he lay on the floor, blaming him for calling his brother and telling him the whereabouts of the Shorts.

The picture Anita tried to paint was of Matty James the puppet master, orchestrating the assassination by telling a man he knew hated the Shorts into murderous action and then 'bragging' about his role.

Anita Cregan blamed Matty James for all the bloodshed that summer, even his son's murder of two police officers.

None of the killings would have happened without Matty James' intervention, she said.

She described how she drove a drunk and apologetic James

home to Clayton, with blood all over his face from the beating dished out by her eldest son.

She said: "He knew what was going to go on between the Shorts and my son. He knew the trouble Dale had had... He just can't keep his mouth shut about anything he's ever been involved in.

"That's what gets him in trouble. He can instigate things and walk away from it and lets everybody else pick up the consequences and brag about it later. I think if he didn't make that phone call... he knew what was going to happen between David Short and Dale one day. He knew. He instigated that night.

"If that night wouldn't have happened, neither would anything else. He may not have had a gun but he caused it all. He knew he had done wrong.

"Dale's one of those people, you can't call his friends. I have never mentioned anything. I had my opinions from day one about Matty James. He made that phone call.

"None of us would be in this courtroom now if he hadn't done that.

"If I had said it to Dale weeks ago, he would have said 'mum, mind your own business and keep quiet'. So I haven't said anything. I'm angry at Matty James. He has started telling lies."

Of course, Tim Ryder, QC for James, jumped to his client's defence and denied that James was the orchestrator of anything.

He was in the wrong pub at the wrong time, that was all.

The only mistakes James had made were being in the Cotton Tree on the night Dale Cregan went looking for the Short family and also picking the phone up when Cregan rang him.

JUSTICE

JERMAINE WARD

Jermaine Ward, the getaway driver after the David Short murder, had an association with Cregan that dated back to at least August, 2009.

Then, Ward was driving a Ford Fiesta registered in Cregan's name when it was stopped by police who found £2,155 in the centre console.

Ward claimed he had borrowed half of it from his mum and the rest was wages from a job at a local garage, but officially he had not declared any income for the previous 18 months.

Police believed it was criminal cash and the courts agreed. Magistrates later ordered the money to be forfeited.

He removed his shoes while he gave evidence during the murder trial to make himself look smaller.

He changed his hairstyle too, with a nerdy side-parting.

In Ward's world and in his words, nothing was his fault. It had all been down to Cregan's bullying threats.

He reckoned that handing himself to police in Huddersfield proved that he was an innocent man and that he had never wished to become involved in the murder of David Short.

As the grilling in court became ever more intense, Ward blurted out: "Sometimes I wish they would have killed me. My family have been going through hell. I was tortured in the mind. I know what happened to me. You wasn't there... I haven't got no involvement in this offence. I have told the police everything. I was bullied into it. I was misled and bullied by Dale Cregan. It's not a good position to be in. It's scary and horrible."

HONOUR AMONG THIEVES

Neither the attempt at a 'little boy lost' makeover nor the tears fooled anyone. If Ward realised he had to do everything to try and save his skin, so too did Irish Immie.

MOHAMMED IMRAN ALI

Mohammed Imran Ali – or Irish Immie – made no secret of the string of women with whom he had casual sex, nor his life of crime.

And it had been some life of crime.

Aged just 15, he received a three-month custodial sentence for two assaults and violent disorder when he appeared at Oldham youth court.

He joined a gang of pupils in a raid on a rival school. One of the victims was hit with a hammer. On another occasion, he battered a 58-year-old man with a plank, although he called it a 'stick' in court. He had also been cautioned in 1995 for burglary, drug trafficking matters and criminal damage. He was handed 42 months in a Young Offenders' Institution for drug trafficking.

As soon as he came out, he was at it again. In 2001, when the police saw him driving erratically on Fields New Road in Chadderton – close to his home – they chased him and stopped him. He tossed an M&M's tub out of the window stuffed with half-a-kilo of heroin worth around £9,000.

He told police the drugs were for his own use. Although he was a drug user, he certainly couldn't use all that. A year later he was handed a four-year jail sentence for drug trafficking.

When he was eventually released again, it didn't take him long to continue dealing in drugs.

Unfortunately for him, he was dealing with an undercover police officer. Ali was handed a seven-year jail sentence in 2004 for supplying heroin and cocaine. He was also handed a further 12 months in prison for breaching the terms of his release licence for the earlier offence.

In all, he had been given jail sentences totalling 16 years by the time Cregan recruited him for the murder of David Short.

After his latest stint behind bars, Irish Immie claimed to have left behind the perilous life of a drug dealer, although he had not exactly gone straight.

This time the trade was in other illicit goods. And if it wasn't nailed down, Irish Immie would flog it. He traded in stolen Next gear which he accepted had 'fallen off the back of a lorry', counterfeit designer clothes, Ugg boots and GHD hair straighteners.

When he wasn't dealing in stolen or fake gear, he was happy to pedal steroids – sometimes for his gym-monster friends inside prison – and Viagra. If there was 'a drink' in it, Immie would sell it.

He also got involved in the security business, co-owning a firm called Lukeman which had 68 bouncers on its books. It folded within two years after it had been 'tarnished' by a rival firm, according to Ali. He used his ready supply of muscle-bound doormen to settle disputes.

He described himself as a 'security consultant' although 'enforcer' would be more accurate. If someone wasn't paying up, Irish Immie could help. He had come to England from Pakistan aged six or seven and had never held down a legitimate job or contributed national insurance, although he had claimed job seeker's allowance.

Cregan had no hesitation in calling Ali to transport him out of Manchester to safety after the murder.

Within a few minutes of getting the call, Irish Immie was in his silver, leased VW Golf and heading south from his home in Chadderton to Failsworth, where the three assassins were getting cleaned up at Press 2 Impress.

The fact he had never taken a driving test let alone held a driving licence didn't stop him from being a getaway driver.

A car leased in his ex-wife's name made sure he wouldn't be stopped while he was out on the roads. He took his three passengers to Bradford where a family friend and property developer – a man named as Raj Khan in court – agreed to take over, putting the men into his BMW X5 and taking them to the Faroe Building.

Ali would continue to drive to and from Leeds over the next few days to make sure the assassins were well stocked up as they kept a low profile.

During the trial, Ali turned on his friend Ward, perhaps under orders from Cregan – furious that Ward had spoken to the police – and perhaps because he didn't want to be seen for what he was – a trusted lieutenant of Cregan.

He claimed it wasn't Cregan who had called him but Ward and that it was actually Ward who had flagged him down when he arrived on Lord Lane in Failsworth.

Ali feigned surprise in court that two strangers – Cregan and Wilkinson – got into his car.

He gave a performance that was full of bravado and bluster as he stood on the witness stand for two days.

Ward seemed 'anxious and panicky' on the phone and had asked for help with a 'spot of bother, according to Ali. He didn't ask what the 'spot of bother' was and simply went to help a friend in need, he claimed. Ward was always getting into trouble and getting into debt he could not repay. He assumed it was another debt and went to help.

He was 'annoyed' when the two others jumped into the car with Ward but didn't say anything as it would have been 'a bit rude'.

He claimed only to have learned that the trio had been involved in the murder of David Short when he saw Cregan's picture on the news later that night. But even he struggled to explain why – having driven back home to Chadderton after dropping his passengers in Bradford – he made another trip to the laundry Press 2 Impress and then a second trip to Bradford that night.

His meek story was that he wanted to apologise to Raj Khan for getting him involved in helping murderers escape.

The truth was Ali needed to make the second trip because Cregan had left behind his bag of munitions at Press 2 Impress, either by mistake or by design, and it needed to be transported to west Yorkshire before the police got their hands on it.

Police finally tracked down Irish Immie a few days after the murders of PCs Fiona Bone and Nichola Hughes.

HONOUR AMONG THIEVES

After he was arrested, police could barely believe what they saw. Ali was covered in tattoos, including pictures of guns and grenades. There was a tattoo of an AK47 rifle with the letters 'TRU' written over it. He claimed it had symbolic meaning in the area of Pakistan where his mother lived. There were also tattoos of silver revolvers across his back which appeared to have angel wings attached. Elsewhere were engravings of a grave with his brother's name on it and hand grenades. He brushed off questions in court and matter-of-factly boasted he had 'hi' tattooed on his penis. Tattoos were 'quite addictive' and he claimed he simply liked the designs.

"I don't think Mr Cregan's pistols have angel wings on them," he said sarcastically.

Ali often took the same nonchalant approach when in the witness box. It did not convince.

ANTHONY WILKINSON

Amid the confusing testimonies and the fog of mistruths, one of Cregan's cohorts actually came clean.

In April, Anthony Wilkinson – the man who gunned down David Short along with Cregan – changed his plea to guilty.

Wilkinson, who had of course sped away to Yorkshire alongside Cregan, Ward and Irish Immie after the crime, realised the game was up.

Just as he had had enough of life on the run, he also saw the futility of trying to argue that he had not murdered David Short.

JUSTICE

However, he remained adamant that he was not guilty of causing an explosion with a grenade and the attempted murder of Sharon Hark just nine minutes after Short was blasted to death.

He therefore remained on trial for those crimes.

All in all, the sheer number of people accused and the plethora of different crimes, motives and locations ensured that the trial was complex, complicated, intense and drawn-out.

Neither the swathes of prosecution lawyers or their opposite numbers on the various defence teams were likely to forget this case in a hurry.

And, of course, there were three grieving families all hoping and waiting to see Cregan get what he deserved.

Finally, after nearly three months of statements, arguments, deliberations and witnesses, the jury were ready to provide verdicts.

Justice was about to be done.

18.

JUSTICE

"Dale Cregan, Stand Up."

On the 77th day of a trial, it was time to draw a line under one of the most shocking series of murders in British criminal history.

Outside Preston Crown Court, it was a beautiful June day. Inside Courtroom Number One, the atmosphere was charged.

It had just gone 4pm when Dale Cregan, wearing a grey sweatshirt, got to his feet in the dock as Mr Justice Holroyde had ordered.

He folded his arms, stroked his chin and smirked. Whether the relaxed demeanour was an affectation or real, only he knew. He was surrounded by 18 security officers.

With his good right eye, he could see through the security glass as the bewigged judge read from his script.

JUSTICE

Just a few yards away in the public gallery sat the grieving friends and relatives of his four murder victims.

Earlier, there had been gasps from Michelle Kelly, the long-time partner of David Short, when the nerveless foreman of the jury stood and delivered the first of his verdicts.

"We find the defendant Leon Atkinson not guilty," he boomed.

Atkinson had not orchestrated the killing of Mark Short in the Cotton Tree.

The furore from the public gallery subsided and the verdicts kept coming.

Francis Dixon shouted 'yes' when he was cleared. The jurors were unaware he was already serving a life sentence and had been on licence at the time of the David Short murder.

On July 10, 2000, he was handed a life sentence for conspiracy to commit armed robbery and carrying firearms. He had been part of a gang of robbers who had led police on a 60-mile chase resulting in the shooting of five innocent passers-by.

Another was held hostage and one police officer was shot. Dixon, who had not fired any shots that day, only served about eight years of his life sentence before being allowed out on licence.

As well as Dixon and Atkinson, also cleared were the alleged spotters for the Cotton Tree assassination: Cregan's best friend, Ryan Hadfield, and the hated Matthew James.

Atkinson, Hadfield and James all walked out of court free men, although they would be urged by the police to think carefully about their personal security.

JUSTICE

The fact they had been cleared certainly didn't mean the threat from the Short clan had disappeared.

They were all marked men.

Matty James had cause to be particularly concerned. By giving evidence against Cregan, he had ensured that he was now a target for both sides.

Dixon's courtroom celebrations were particularly premature. He had been recalled to prison as the murder charge which he had just defeated meant he had breached his early release clause.

He would face a parole board hearing where he would have to convince another panel that his confessed association with a convicted mass murderer was an innocent one.

The jury foreman continued with the verdicts.

Luke Livesey: guilty.

Damian Gorman: guilty.

Jermaine Ward: guilty.

Mohammed Imran Ali: guilty.

There were more not guilty verdicts but these were academic. Cregan was acquitted of the one count he continued to deny: a charge that he had attempted to murder Sharon Hark.

His barristers had successfully argued that if he had meant to kill her, she would be dead.

The grenade he had thrown at her house was merely a warning.

The jurors agreed and found him innocent of that charge. Sharon Hark may not have thought so, but it was a pretty meaningless decision as Cregan had already confessed to all the other charges at points during the trial: four murders, three attempted murders and causing an explosion with a hand grenade.

However, Cregan will have savoured the fact he had not been found guilty on any charge.

As he had demonstrated during his killing spree, he liked things on his own terms.

And so it was with his guilt or otherwise in court, all of which he had decided.

His henchman for the David Short murder, Anthony Wilkinson, could also draw on a similar crumb of comfort as the jurors found him not guilty of attempting to murder Sharon Hark and causing the hand grenade explosion outside her house.

As the acquitted men were escorted out of the dock, Cregan smiled and shook them by the their hands, one by one.

His gym partner Atkinson, best friend Hadfield and mentor Dixon all received his hearty congratulations as they were led out of court.

Matty James was given the cold-shoulder.

Michelle Kelly and other members of the Short family struggled to conceal their anger and disappointment as these four men walked out, three of them to their freedom.

They weren't alone.

On a row behind them, the detectives who had led the murder investigations sat grim-faced.

The job of keeping the peace in east Manchester just got that much harder.

Remaining in the dock with Cregan were his partners in

crime: Luke Livesey, Damian Gorman, Anthony Wilkinson, Jermaine Ward and Mohammed Imran Ali.

They were about to learn their fate. Just how lengthy would their sentences be?

Cregan sat there, the very epitome of indifference as his junior counsel, Michael Lavery, offered not a single word in mitigation for his client.

It seemed Cregan had nothing to say, which was typical of his attitude towards the entire trial.

However, well-placed sources at court revealed how Cregan, in the cells below court, made it clear he had wanted his lawyer to speak up on his behalf.

Not to extend an olive branch though.

He had urged the barrister to tell the court he wished he had killed more people during his murder spree.

Cregan knew he was never likely to leave jail, never likely to get another public platform in which to hail his contempt for the Shorts, the police and almost everyone in between.

He had wanted to go down screaming, with his quotes and his thoughts splashed across the national papers. In the end, this never happened.

It was perhaps as well his attitude was never made public.

In the dock, Cregan appeared unconcerned as he waited to hear his sentence.

Mr Justice Holroyde, who would no doubt have been unsurprised to hear of Cregan's continuing belligerence behind the scenes, wasted little time dealing with the one-eyed killer before him, first describing the murders of Mark Short and the 'man you hated' David Short before moving on to the 'quite appalling' slaughter of PCs Bone and Hughes: "You lured two female police officers to their deaths by making a false report that you have been a victim of crime.

"I have no doubt you were expecting one or more unarmed officers to attend, and that is what happened. You had armed yourself with at least one grenade and with a self-loading pistol to which you had fitted an extended magazine containing 32 rounds.

"PC Fiona Bone and PC Nicola Hughes were sent in response to your call for help, performing their public duty for the public good. From your position within the house, I have no doubt you were able to see them coming and you must have seen that they were unarmed female officers.

"You opened the front door and, with the advantage of surprise, you opened fire before your victims had any chance to do anything to protect themselves. The analysis made by an expert witness who visited the scene was chilling evidence. "Although the officers survived the first shots which hit them, you pursued them with a cold-blooded and ruthless determination to end their lives.

"One of your shots struck PC Hughes in the back, with the result she lay on the ground paralysed. You left her there and pursued PC Bone, firing some 20 shots at her. You then returned to PC Hughes and made sure you killed her by shooting her in the head.

"Finally, not content with what you had already done, you exploded another hand grenade near the body of PC Hughes, inflicting yet further injuries.

JUSTICE

"You acted with premeditated savagery... You drew those two officers into a calculated trap for the sole purpose of murdering them in cold blood."

Despite its rather quaint appearance, a criminal court can be the most brutal and inhospitable place on earth.

Each successive word from the judge pierced the already broken hearts of the officers' families watching from the public gallery.

And their discomfort wasn't over yet.

They had penned 'victim personal statements' describing in detail how their lives had been shattered.

The judge had read each one alone in his chambers before coming into court.

He read others from members of the Short family, including the three men who had been shot but survived the CottonTree hit.

These highly personal documents weren't for public consumption.

They didn't need to be.

In measured terms, Mr Justice Holroyde gave a brief outline of the anguish of Cregan's victims about which he had just read.

His words allowed everyone in court to see for themselves the shadow cast by a terrible ogre.

No-one had to see the monster itself to understand a little of the continuing pain and grief being felt by Cregan's victims.

"The statements" said the judge as he continued to address Cregan "spell out the reality of witnessing the murder of a child or loved one; the reality of the grim duty of identifying the body of a child or loved one, in two of these cases in the knowledge that the deceased has been has been disfigured by the explosion of a grenade; the reality of living as a parent bereaved of a child, noting as the years go by each anniversary or event which the deceased child had not lived to enjoy; the reality of living as a parent of a bewildered young child, trying to explain why the deceased will not come home and will not answer a phone call."

As he spoke, PC Hughes' father, Bryn, embraced his weeping wife, Natalie.

Words which could hardly fail to move any parent barely registered with Dale Cregan.

They simply washed over him as he sat in his seat in the dock, arrogant and cocksure.

"Dale Cregan, stand up," the judge ordered.

He casually got to his feet. Perhaps he recognised the phrase 'whole life order' as he finally learned his fate.

Nine months earlier, he had been sitting in Alan Whitwell's front room in Abbey Gardens when he Googled 'life sentence' on the family laptop while his hostages cowered upstairs.

He knew back then that this moment of reckoning would come.

"The court is driven to the conclusion that there must be a whole life order.

"That means, in plain terms, that you will never be released from prison," the judge told him, and Cregan was taken down.

19.

ROT IN HELL

The news that Cregan would never be released from prison was flashed around the world.

Sky, BBC, ITV and Channel 4 all had presenters at the foot of the steps of Preston Crown Court telling audiences in grave tones what no-one ever doubted – that Cregan would die in prison. It was scant consolation for his victims. It was understandable some wanted Cregan to be hoisted to the nearest gallows to see him swing for his crimes. Once they had gathered themselves, they spoke with a mix of dignity and anger about their loss and the crimes committed by Cregan and his cohorts.

For the record, Cregan was handed six life sentences.

For the three attempted murders in the Cotton Tree, he attracted a minimum term in prison of 11 years before he could apply for parole.

JUSTICE

For exploding a grenade outside Sharon Hark's home, he was told he had to serve at least six years.

These sentences were all legal niceties as, for each of the four murders he had committed, the judge said he would never be eligible for release.

Anthony Wilkinson was given life for the murder of David Short and told he could only apply for parole after 34 years, by which time he will be 77 years old. For possessing the Browning 9mm found at his mum's house, he got six years behind bars.

Jermaine Ward was also given life for the murder of Short snr and told it would be 33 years before he could apply for release. By then, he will be 57.

Damien Gorman was sentenced to life for killing Mark Short and for the attempted murders of three others. He will serve 33 years before he is eligible for parole. By then he will be 72.

Luke Livesey was found guilty on the same charges as Gorman and must also serve a minimum of 33 years. He will be 61 before he can apply for parole.

Mohammed Imran Ali – Irish Immie – was the only convicted defendant who didn't get a life sentence. He was jailed for seven years for the crime of assisting an offender. The maximum sentence for that crime was 10 years.

The length of the sentences reflected the nation's horror at the crimes.

The message from the justice system could not have been any clearer. Launching killing sprees, gunning down people in pubs, and murdering police officers in cold blood would never be tolerated.

Finally, it was time for the villains involved to disappear as their victims' families continued to try and come to terms with their respective losses.

PC Nicola Hughes' father, Bryn, like many after him, never mentioned Cregan in his statement outside court.

It was part of a general effort by his victims to airbrush the man who had ruined their lives out of history.

It was both tragic and heroic.

He said: "Tuesday, September 18, 2012, is a day that will remain burned on our hearts and minds forever. Nicola left for work that morning like any other morning, in the expectation that she would return home at the end of her shift. We were ripped apart beyond belief that day, nothing could have prepared us for the utter devastation we were about to endure for no reason other than the fact that Nicola was a police officer. She was brutally and callously murdered in the most despicable and cowardly way.

"We can only imagine what thoughts and feelings she experienced in those few seconds it took for this person to pull the trigger and for Nicola to draw her last breath.

"Our lives have been shattered beyond belief and will never be the same again, to have a child taken from you in such a cruel and meaningless way is without doubt the worst thing any parent can wish to imagine. The amount of people affected by Nicola's death is a measure of how popular and loved she was by her family, friends and colleagues alike. Thankfully, as a result of the whole life tariff imposed by the courts, this person will never experience freedom again.

JUSTICE

"There are other people who should also bear some responsibility for the deaths of Nicola and Fiona, those people who harboured and assisted this person while he was at large following the equally horrific murders that led to the deaths of Nicola and Fiona.

"They should be thoroughly ashamed of themselves."

The Hughes' family continued in a joint statement: "Nicola embraced everything she did throughout her life with total commitment and enthusiasm. She touched the hearts of everyone she came into contact with and who were part of her life. In September, 2012, she was at her happiest.

"She was a very proud and dedicated police officer. She had a career that she loved and enjoyed, with colleagues, who she often called friends. She was planning her future with her boyfriend, Gareth, and had just become the proud godmother of Jack. She had so much to look forward to, a bright future, one she had worked hard for and one she deserved to live to the full.

"Nicola's life was snatched away from her on the morning of Tuesday, September 18, when she, and her colleague Fiona... answered a routine call to an address in Hattersley. This call turned into anything but a routine call and transformed the lives of everyone involved: for Nicola and Fiona whose lives were taken away in the most unnecessary and brutal of circumstances; for her family and friends who lost the most beautiful, fun loving and dedicated young woman that ever lived; for the officers and staff of Greater Manchester Police who lost a valued colleague, partner and friend.

"As for the man convicted of her murder – he has lost nothing.

"He had already committed two murders and was destined for a lifetime behind bars. He chose, on that day, to murder our daughter and leave our lives completely devastated, a life barely worth living without her. Now the trial has concluded he will return to his cell to live the rest of his natural life. We, however, will live with what he did every single hour of every single day for the rest of our lives.

"It is beyond our understanding how and why anyone would want to murder two innocent young women who were doing their jobs and had arrived with nothing but thoughts of providing assistance to someone in need of their help. Our whole lives will always surround what happened on that day. Birthdays, Christmas and anniversaries are now lost to memories and will never ever be the same again. Our lives will always be so empty without her."

They concluded: "As for the man who took our beautiful, devoted daughter, sister and girlfriend away from us, we hope he remains incarcerated for the rest of his life, that he may never, ever, inflict such pain and suffering on anyone ever again."

Typically, PC Fiona Bone's father, Paul Bone, used the occasion to look outwards to console other victims rather than inwards, expressing relief that her daughter's colleagues had been spared the ordeal of reliving the murder in court and extending a hand of sympathy to PC Hughes' and the Short families. The police, court staff, prosecutors and the judge and jurors were all thanked for their efforts in 'what must have been a difficult case.

JUSTICE

He said: "My family is still coming to terms with our loss and not a day goes by without thinking of Fiona. I am told that it gets easier in time but, for the moment, every Tuesday lunchtime is difficult, for that was when our lives changed forever. Yes, we have regrets that Fiona was taken from us but we have no regrets that she was a police officer with Greater Manchester Police and we are extremely proud of her life and achievements."

Chief Supt Nick Adderley, the dead officers' boss at the Tameside subdivision of GMP, wore his heart on his sleeve: "No amount of time behind bars for those responsible is going to ease the pain and sense of loss that the loved ones of Nicola, Fiona and the Short family will feel for the rest of their lives, but the sentences handed down mean that the corrosive influences and effects of these vile individuals on others, has been halted.

"Following the murders of Fiona and Nicola, the response from communities across Tameside and Clayton has been overwhelming, as has the support from across the world. This once again highlights that these parasites, who feed off the hard working and vulnerable, are a mere spec of insignificance in the grand scheme of humanity and that their removal from society will be celebrated by most, and missed by few.

"Often criminals live with the misconception they somehow 'own' turf, territory and people, believing they bring their own rule of law, but quite the opposite is true. Since the events of last year, the community has become fitter, stronger, more unified and more determined than ever to stand against those who tear good people and families apart.

"Our efforts have intensified and many more criminals have been arrested and assets seized as a direct consequence of the collaboration between the police, public and our partner agencies, and for that I am extremely grateful. As a policing community, we continue to recover, never forgetting the sacrifice and the immense bravery of our departed friends and colleagues, Nicola Hughes and Fiona Bone. Bravery that most of us could only ever imagine possible, yet dare to believe would ever be necessary."

Insp Ian Hanson, the chairman of the Greater Manchester branch of the Police Federation, and PC Bone's old inspector, was characteristically outspoken: "Police officers often speak to the media in relation to horrific events and usually we manage to suppress our feelings and speak with a degree of controlled emotion in conveying our message. I am not going to allow myself that luxury.

"Instead, I am going to say precisely what our murdered friends' colleagues think and what I firmly believe the decent people of Greater Manchester think too.

"Dale Cregan is an abomination upon our society and, in my view, he has forfeited the right to walk the streets for the rest of his life. I hope that he dies in prison many years from now a sad, lonely old man, having spent decades staring at a cell door, after which, as far as I am concerned, he can rot in hell for all eternity. If people think that's harsh, then I am afraid they are just going to have to live with it.

"The difference between Cregan and Nicola Hughes and Fiona Bone is that he will quickly be reduced to being a nobody and, in years to come, no-one will even know his name. However the names of Constables Nicola Hughes and Fiona Bone will be forever remembered in GMP history as being two brave colleagues who gave their young lives simply because they wanted to make Greater Manchester a better place.

"God bless them and may they now rest in peace."

Meanwhile, the Short family spoke darkly about the 'cowards' and 'animals' who had murdered David and Mark Short.

It was clear they were still fuelled by grief at the shattering loss of both men.

Just a few days earlier, as the jurors were still considering their verdicts, someone had taken a hammer to David Short's grave in Droylsden Cemetery.

Flowers and pictures of him had been scattered all around the plot and his headstone had been damaged. Stark police intelligence suggested Cregan's allies on the outside would dig up the Shorts and hang their bodies in the street.

The anger between the two sides was clear and for many police officers, it was a case of when and not if there was more bloodshed.

One source said: "Mark my words. This isn't the end of the story."

Outside Preston Crown Court, David Short's still grieving partner Michelle Kelly, the mother of Mark Short, had her statement read out: "The 25th of May, 2012, was the day that my life turned into a living nightmare. A nightmare that I am still living and will be for the rest of my life. I will never stop crying. Mark and David didn't just die, they were brutally murdered by cowards. Dave and I were there when Mark was murdered. We witnessed the murder of our only son something that will haunt me forever. Mark has a three-year-old son, Mark Junior, and a loving partner, Naomi. They had a future together. They had plans for that future."

She described how she had only been in work a couple of hours when she learned 'Dave had been shot'.

She continued: "It was only 11 weeks after losing my son. It was totally devastating. They have not only taken my son Mark from me, they have now taken my Dave as well. I have been with Dave for 28 years. We had two wonderful children together, three beautiful grandchildren.

"They were together in life and are now together in spirit. Dave gave and received from his son 23 years of love. Me and my family shared that love and that is something that I will always treasure. The love of Dave and Mark will always be with me. They could not beat Dave in life and they will not beat him in death. We are happy with the sentences given out to the ones convicted. We are not happy with the total outcome of the verdicts."

David Short's daughter, Stacey – Mark Short's sister – said: "No-one should have to go through what me and my family have been through. We were a happy family and now half my family have been taken away from me. My dad and brother will never be forgotten. They will always be in our hearts and memories. No-one can take them away."

She pointed to Cregan's henchmen and said: "It would have only taken one of them to have prevented what happened to both my brother and my father. One of them could have called the police anonymously and stopped all this from happening. I don't know how they can live with themselves.

"I truly hope they rot in hell."

As his many victims had their say, Dale Cregan was on his way to Full Sutton high security prison to the east of York to spend the rest of his days.

They will not be easy days.

Despite his self-professed toughness and reputation for savagery, Cregan knows he will have to constantly remain vigilant against revenge attacks.

Police intelligence has indicated that the head of southern-based gypsy family has placed a £20,000 bounty, not to kill Cregan, but to blind him by gouging out his good right eye.

He must now spend the rest of his life looking over his shoulder, terrified in the knowledge he could be blinded at any second.

Of course, that will not be enough to help assuage the grief and anger prompted by his terrible actions across the summer of 2012.

Nothing can undo his actions, nothing can bring back Mark Short, David Short or PCs Nicola Hughes and Fiona Bone.

However, if the £20,000 is paid out, and Cregan's sadistic mind is plunged into darkness, he will get all the sympathy he deserves.

None.